The "EASY WAY" Series

~~HARD~~ EASY ~~HAR-~~DOS IT!

(Part 2 of Easy DOS It!)

by Ron Bauer

Illustrated by
Sandra Kort

published by

the EASY WAY PRESS, inc.
ELECTRONIC PUBLISHERS

P.O. Box 906 ✦ Rochester, MI 48308-0906
Phone: (313) 651 - 9405

Hard DOS It!
Second Edition

TRADEMARK ACKNOWLEDGEMENTS:

IBM is a trademark of International Business Machines Corp.
Compaq is a trademark of Compaq Computer Corp.
Macintosh is a trademark of Apple Computer, Inc.
LaserWriter is a trademark of Apple Computer, Inc.
Word is a trademark of Microsoft
Microsoft Press is a trademark of Microsoft
MS-DOS is a trademark of Microsoft
PC-DOS is a trademark of IBM
PageMaker is a trademark of Aldus Corp.
Sentinel is a trademark of Sentinel Technologies
PC to MAC and BACK is a trademark of dilithium Press

This booklet was written using Microsoft Word
Text was transferred from a Compaq using PC to MAC and BACK
The illustrations were produced using Macintosh software
Layout produced with PageMaker

Library of Congress Cataloging-in-Publication Data

Bauer, Ron, 1938-
    Hard DOS it!

    ("The Learn in a day way!" series)
    1. PC DOS (Computer operating system) 2. MS-DOS
(Computer operating system) I. Title. II. Title: Hard
does it! III. Series.
QA76.76.063B395 1988   005.4'469   88-31078
ISBN 0-942019-05-9

Printed in the United States of America

20 19 18 17 16 15 14 13

READ THIS FIRST

If you're a person who wants to get started using a hard disk the easy way, this book's for you. Before reading it, though, learn the material covered in chapters one through seven in the *Easy DOS It!* book. Those chapters introduce you to the routine and repetitive DOS operations you *need to know* to use any MS- or PC- DOS personal computer.

If you happen to be someone who went through all eleven chapters of *Easy DOS It!* before getting this book, you didn't waste your time. All eleven commands covered are essential for using floppy disks, which are essential to a hard disk computer. That's how they got their name — the "Essential Eleven."

There are a few more commands to learn for using a hard disk — but only eight. After much thought and deliberation, I decided to call the eight additional comands the "Additional Eight." (Can it be that too much computerese dampens creativity?)

Now get started having some fun learning to master the hard disk in your personal computer.

Ron Bauer
September, 1987

CONTENTS

PREPARE DISKS

Blank Disks

Blank disks are blank.

That's not so self-evident as it sounds. In computerese, disks are either...

1. Blank.

2. Blank, but formatted.

This is computerese because blank should be *blank*, and in this instance it isn't. But, let's not quibble. Let's investigate the differences.

DOS provides a command called FORMAT. Its function is to prepare disks to conform to your disk drives. Disks must be prepared with this command before you can store files on them.

Jim Kelsh of Central Michigan University, a computer scientist, compares a computer to a child. He analogizes a blank disk to a blank sheet of paper; a formatted disk to a lined sheet of paper. The child needs the lines before he or she can begin to write (in a legible manner). Interesting.

Before I show you how to format blank disks for DOS, take the precaution to protect your master DOS disk. Check that it's write protected.

Write Protect

You can write protect floppy disks. When you write protect a disk, the read/write head can't write on it. A write protected disk is safe from accidental, or deliberate, erasure. The methods for write protecting floppy and micro floppy disks differ slightly, even though the results are the same.

Make sure your master DOS disk is write protected now. If it's a floppy, and has an open write protect notch, the large notch at the edge of the disk near the label, wrap a self-adhesive write protect tab around it...

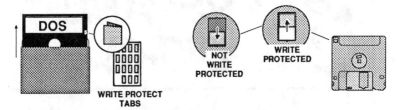

If it's a micro floppy, use the built-in write protect tab. When the tab's in the open position, the disk is write protected. It's the opposite of the floppy disk which is NOT write protected when the notch is open. (I wonder who made THAT decision?!)

The Two Drive System

Computers with hard disks are, typically, two drive systems. One drive is a floppy or micro floppy, the other a hard disk. Each drive has a different name.

The floppy, or micro floppy, drive is the A: drive, the hard disk drive is the C: drive. The designation, B: drive, is customarily used for a second floppy, or micro floppy, drive. Note that drive names include colons.

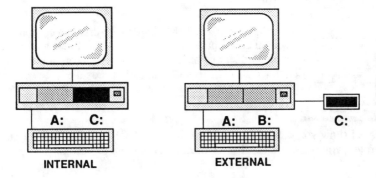

Any computer can be transformed into a hard disk system either by replacing one of two floppy drives with an internal hard disk, or by adding an external hard disk.

The only drives we'll be concerned about in this book, regardless of the setup you might be using, are the A: and C: drives.

The FORMAT Command

All blank disks must be prepared before they can hold files. In this chapter, we'll prepare three floppy disks, then one hard disk. The preparing procedure for floppy disks is simply a matter of running each disk through the DOS program called FORMAT.

FORMAT analyzes a disk for defective tracks, generates a directory, sets up file allocations, and makes other technical modifications. DOS does it, not you. You do the easy part.

Before you begin, though, prepare three labels. On the first, print "BLANK FORMATTED." On the second, print "BLANK FORMATTED WITH SYSTEM." On the third, print "DOS WORKING COPY." Put one label on each of the three blank disks mentioned in Chapter One.

One precaution you should always take before using the FORMAT command is to check the directory of any disk you suspect may contain some data. That's because FORMAT erases everything on the disk. Any important data would be lost. Do it now with the disk labelled "BLANK FORMATTED." Put it in the A: drive, and close the door. Type **DIR**, and press the **[ENTER]** key...

```
A>DIR
Disk error reading in drive A
Abort, Retry, Ignore? _
```

The "disk error" message usually means there's no formatting. But, it *could* mean wrong formatting or a damaged disk, too. I'll assume the disk is blank. Type A for Abort, bringing you back to the system prompt.

A similar message to the above is...

```
Not ready error reading in drive A
Abort, Retry, Ignore? _
```

This message usually means you left the drive door open. Leaving a drive door open does no harm. If you ever forget to close the drive door, put things right by closing it, then pressing **R** for Retry.

WARNING

When the red light on a drive is glowing, the internal mechanisms of the drive are active. WAIT UNTIL THE LIGHT GOES OFF before touching the door, or removing or inserting a disk. If it doesn't go off in one or two minutes, boot your computer again.

Replace the disk in the A: drive with the DOS disk. Then, enter the FORMAT command by typing **FORMAT**, and pressing the **[ENTER]** key...

```
A>FORMAT
Drive letter must be specified

A>_
```

Oops! It didn't work. That's because DOS requires a parameter for the FORMAT command. As with the DIR command, you specify a drive with a drive specifying parameter. (Parameter was defined in Chapter Seven, page 34.)

> *NOTE: Earlier versions of DOS will not require the drive specifier.*

Enter the FORMAT command again. This time include the drive specifying parameter. Type **FORMAT A:**, and press the **[ENTER]** key...

```
A>FORMAT A:
Insert new diskette for drive A
and strike ENTER when ready _
```

Replace the DOS disk with the disk labelled "BLANK FORMATTED." When ready, "strike ENTER" which means the same as press the **[ENTER]** key...

```
Formatting...
```

Wait a few moments as the program works. (This technical stuff is tough!) Some versions of DOS help you pass the time by displaying the Head/Cylinder running count. You may watch if you wish, but it will do it anyway. When the formatting is complete, you see...

```
Formatting..Format complete

        362496 bytes total disk space
        362496 bytes available on disk

Format another (Y/N)? _
```

Press **N** for *No*. Then press the [ENTER] key, leaving the FORMAT program, and returning to the system prompt.

> *It's possible that FORMAT may detect some errors. If it does, you'll see a message telling you there are "bytes in bad sectors." Try formatting again. If the bad sector message is still there, I recommend you use a different disk, or you may eventually have trouble.*

This disk is now considered "a blank, formatted disk" as opposed to "a blank disk." I'm still curious about this paradoxical use of the term blank. I can only suspect that the guy who came up with the term *boot* is involved. There's no way to prove it, though.

You check for formatting the same way you check for files. Look at the directory. Type **DIR**, and press the [ENTER] key...

```
A>DIR
 Volume in drive A has no label
 Directory of A:\

File not found

A> _
```

As you can see, the "official" message shows that DOS now has something it can read. In this case, it reads and finds no files, then returns to the system prompt because everything's okay.

By the way, don't worry about "volume labels." This book makes DOS easy to learn because it doesn't waste your time on irrelevant explanations. If you want some, though, some *other* information I mean, read your DOS manual.

Formatted With System

Replace the disk in the A: drive with the DOS disk. Close the door. This time type **FORMAT A:/S**, and press the [ENTER] key...

```
A>FORMAT A:/S
Insert new diskette for drive A:
and strike ENTER when ready _
```

Replace your DOS disk with the disk labelled "BLANK FORMATTED WITH SYSTEM." Press (or strike) the [ENTER] key...

```
Formatting..Format complete

        362496 bytes total disk space
         62464 bytes used by system
        300032 bytes available on disk

Format another? (Y/N)? _
```

Note that the message now includes "*62464 bytes used by system*" (or more bytes, if you're using a micro floppy). Type **N**, and press the [ENTER] key to get back to the system prompt.

Adding the /S parameter to the FORMAT command switched on a subprogram that copied certain files onto the disk. If you look at the directory of this newly formatted "blank with system" disk, you'll see one file, the COMMAND.COM...

COMMAND.COM... *DOS file containing instructions to carry out DOS commands stored in RAM.*

There are also two or more system files. They don't show up on the directory because they are hidden. Why are they hidden? I don't know. I do know that the system and COMMAND.COM files on a disk are necessary for booting a computer. Other DOS files need not be there, but these do.

Despite the presence of the three or more files on this disk, it's still called "blank" in computerese. Those are the rules. I didn't make them, I'm just informing you.

Replace the "BLANK FORMATTED WITH SYSTEM" disk in the A: drive with the DOS disk. Remember to close the drive door.

The Hard Disk's Turn

When you run the FORMAT command on a disk, floppy or hard, DOS divides up the surfaces. The divisions are concentric circles called TRACKS (recently called CYLINDERS) which are divided again into SECTORS. A standard (360k) floppy disk has 40 sectors. A standard (720k) micro floppy has 80 sectors. Hard disks, depending on their size, begin in the thousands. Naturally, this means it's going to take longer to format a hard disk.

When formatting a hard disk for the first time, some additional preparations may be necessary. These preparations are usually covered by the catch-all computerese term INSTALLATION...

INSTALLATION... *operates ranging from putting hardware into hardware to making software-driven modifications to hardware or software. It's any interfacing (What a word!) of elements in a computer system — hardware, software, or both.*

? Before proceeding, answer the following questions...

1. Do you care about the inner workings of hard disks?
2. Is it necessary to INSTALL your hard disk?

If you answered YES to either question, turn to the APPENDIX.
If you answered NO to both questions, you're ready to proceed.

There are several variations in the preparation of a hard disk, depending on its installation status. If you're unsure of the installation status of your hard disk, one way to check is try to access its directory. In a two drive system, this means you must access the directory of the other drive.

The Other Drive

Since A: is the drive you're working with, C: is the other drive in the system we're using. There are two ways to gain access to the contents of the other drive. One is to use a drive specifying parameter.

Try using the DIR command, specifying the C: drive. Simply type **DIR C:**, and press the **[ENTER]** key...

```
A>DIR C:
Invalid drive specification
```

If you see this message, there's no hard disk called C:, so you'd better check with somebody! Probably, you'll see this...

```
A>DIR C:
Not ready error reading in drive C
Abort, Retry, Ignore? _
```

Such a "disk error" message either means the disk in the C: drive is damaged, or it hasn't been formatted. If it *has* been formatted, the message will look like this...

```
A>DIR C:
 Volume in drive C has no label
 Directory of C:\

File not found

A> _
```

Or, there'll be some files listed, which means someone's used, or is using this hard disk. Some dealers supply hard disks ready-to-use, and include special files and programs for that particular computer. Don't format a disk containing files you want to keep. Why? Because FORMAT will erase them.

Formatting the Hard Disk

The procedure for formatting a hard disk is the same as for preparing a "BLANK FORMATTED WITH SYSTEM" floppy disk. It just takes longer because the hard disk is bigger.

Put the DOS disk in the A: drive. Enter the FORMAT command followed by two parameters, the C: drive specifier and the "system transfer" switch. Type **FORMAT C:/S**, and press the [ENTER] key...

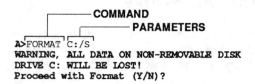

```
              ┌─────── COMMAND
              │   ┌──── PARAMETERS
A>FORMAT  C:/S
WARNING, ALL DATA ON NON-REMOVABLE DISK
DRIVE C: WILL BE LOST!
Proceed with Format (Y/N)?
```

This warning should speak for itself, but, risking redundancy, I'll comment on it. The FORMAT command will erase all data on a disk! So, unless there's data you don't want to lose on the hard disk, press **Y**, then the [ENTER] key...

```
Formatting...
```

Now you wait. While you're waiting, you can take a stretch, look out the window, or, if your version of DOS shows it, stare at the running Head/Cylinder count. DOS is doing all the work.

The reason it takes longer to format a hard disk than a floppy disk is, of course, because of the relative sizes. Even a small hard disk is 30 or more times larger than a floppy disk.

Once the hard disk is formatted, you see the following message...

```
Formatting..Format complete
System transferred
```

It's a good policy to format your hard disk at least once a year. Why? Because scattered data accumulates. Formatting and replacing the data will "freshen" its performance. An alternative to formatting for improved performance is using a utility software program for "optimizing perform- ance." Ask your friendly computer hardware or software supplier about one.

WARNING

Entering C>FORMAT can provide you with a nice, clean hard disk, but no files. FORMAT erases everything, so always check the directory of any disk, especially a hard disk, before running FORMAT.

You can imagine the unhappy feeling of destroying hours of your work. Even worse, you could also destroy the work of vindictive colleagues. That could be fatal!

Hard Disk Test

When you formatted the hard disk, you included the /S parameter. The reason was to prepare the hard disk to boot the computer. Normally, when you boot a computer, DOS looks for system and COMMAND.COM files on the A: drive, and the A> prompt appears. If you leave the A: drive door open, however, DOS will look for the system on the C: drive.

Try it now. Open the A: drive door, then hold down the [CTRL] and [ALT] keys, and press the [DEL] key.

If all is well, the computer boots from the hard disk. The prompts for DATE and TIME are the same as described in Chapter Six, the only difference being that C> rather than A> is the prompt. The C: drive has booted the computer, and become the default drive. You may not be completely sure what that means yet, so let's look at that catchy computerese.

More About Default and Logged Drives

DOS, without specific instructions, will *always* use the DEFAULT DRIVE...

DEFAULT DRIVE... *the logged drive.*

At first look, it may seem like I'm defining one computerese term with another, but that's only because I am. Although both terms were covered in Chapter Six, their practical meaning may have become a bit foggy by now, so here's some help.

The logged drive is where DOS looks for command instructions. If you type a command such as DIR at the A: drive prompt, *by default* you see the directory of the A: drive. DOS uses the logged drive unless you specify another. You can tell which is the logged drive from the system prompt. The prompt is a letter followed by a "greater than" bracket (>), followed by a blinking cursor.

For example, now you're logged onto the C: drive. The C> prompt is the last item on your screen, and has a blinking cursor. With the DOS disk in the A: drive, type A:, and press the [ENTER] key...

    C>A:

    A> _

As you can see, the A> prompt with blinking cursor is now the last item on your screen. A: is the logged drive.

Log back onto the C: drive by reversing the previous procedure. Simply type C: and press the [ENTER] key...

    A>C:

    C> _

Once logged onto a drive, all commands act on it by default. You're logged onto the C: drive now, so type **DIR**, and press the [ENTER] key...

    C>DIR
    Volume in drive C has no label
    Directory of C:\

    COMMAND   COM   23210   3-07-85   1:43p

    C> _

Remember, you can use a drive specifying parameter to see the directory of the other drive, the A: drive. Type **DIR A:**, and press the **[ENTER]** key...

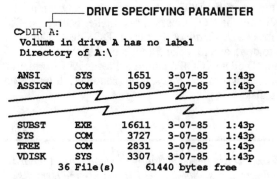

```
                ┌──── DRIVE SPECIFYING PARAMETER
C>DIR A:
 Volume in drive A has no label
 Directory of A:\

 ANSI     SYS      1651    3-07-85    1:43p
 ASSIGN   COM      1509    3-07-85    1:43p


 SUBST    EXE     16611    3-07-85    1:43p
 SYS      COM      3727    3-07-85    1:43p
 TREE     COM      2831    3-07-85    1:43p
 VDISK    SYS      3307    3-07-85    1:43p
         36 File(s)      61440 bytes free

 C> _
```

> ### The Other Drive Rules
>
> *When you're logged onto the A: drive, C: is the other drive.*
> *When you're logged onto the C: drive, A: is the other drive.*

Spaces

When you enter instructions, spaces are critical. The general rules for using spaces when entering commands are simple...

- NO space between drive specifying parameter and filename
- ONE space between command and drive specifying parameter
- NO space before switch parameter

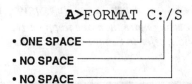

```
            A>FORMAT C:/S

    • ONE SPACE ─────────┘ │  │
    • NO SPACE ─────────────┘  │
    • NO SPACE ────────────────┘
```

> ### BREAK TIME
>
> *Perhaps you want to take a short break here. The following commands should be tried in one sitting. If you're going to continue, don't stop until the end of this chapter.*

The DISKCOPY Command

You've seen some of the ways that DOS is the connection between hardware and software. Without the DOS files, your computer is useless. So, a good precaution is to make a *duplicate* of the master DOS disk. DOS provides an easy way to do it, and to make sure it's done right — the DISKCOPY command. The DISKCOPY command reads ALL formatting and data from one disk, and writes, or copies, it onto another. It makes an *exact* copy of an entire disk.

> *From now on, I'll use the term floppy to mean both standard and micro floppy disks. Sometimes I'll just use the term disk.*

The master DOS disk, containing the DISKCOPY command, is still in the A: drive. If not, put it there. Type **DISKCOPY**, then press the [**ENTER**] key...

```
A> DISKCOPY

Insert source diskette in drive A:

Press any key when ready . . .
_
```

Some versions of DOS need the command entered with drive specifiers (DISKCOPY A: A:).

> *NOTE: The parameters are different for the DISKCOPY command if you're using more than one floppy drive. If you need this information, refer to Chapter Eight of Easy DOS It! for instructions.*

Leave the DOS disk in the A: drive, and press any key. The drive light will glow as DOS reads the contents of the disk into RAM. When it's finished you'll see...

```
Insert target diskette in drive A:

Press any key when ready . . .
_
```

The instructions on your screen tell you what to do next. Replace the DOS disk (or "diskette" as DOS elegantly proclaims) with the one labelled "DOS WORKING COPY." Press any key. You'll see the disk drive light glow, and the following acknowledgement appear on the screen...

```
Copying 40 tracks
9 Sectors/Track, 2 side(s)
```

You can DISKCOPY onto a blank (unformatted) disk because DOS checks for correct formatting before it copies. If necessary, it formats it...

```
Formatting while copying
```

When the DISKCOPY procedure is complete, you'll see...

```
Copy another diskette (Y/N)? _
```

Press **N**, which brings you back to the system prompt. Don't remove the disk from its drive yet.

The DISKCOMP Command

DISKCOPY's purpose is to make an exact copy, but just in case, DOS has a program for comparing every bit and byte of two disks. It's called DISKCOMP (DISK COMPare). You run DISKCOMP the same way you did DISKCOPY. First, DISKCOMP must be on the DOS disk. Type **DISKCOMP**, and press the **[ENTER]** key...

```
A>DISKCOMP

Insert FIRST diskette in drive A:

Press any key when ready . . .
_
```

Some versions of DOS need the command entered with drive specifiers (DISKCOMP A: A:).

It doesn't matter which of the two is the "FIRST diskette" because they're supposed to be identical. However, I begin with the master DOS disk in the A: drive so my instructions are easier to follow. Please do the same. Once it's in place, press any key...

```
Comparing 40 tracks
9 sectors per track, 2 side(s)
```

Soon you see...

```
Insert SECOND diskette in drive A:

Press any key when ready . . .
_
```

Replace the master DOS disk in the A: drive with the "DOS WORKING COPY" disk. Again the disk drive light glows as DOS compares the disks. When complete, the screen *should* say...

```
Compare OK
Compare another diskette (Y/N)? _
```

Press **N** to return to the system prompt.

> *If the disks **don't** compare ok, you didn't get an exact copy. Try DISKCOMP again with the same disks. If the procedure fails a second time, get a new blank disk, and repeat both the DISKCOPY and DISKCOMP procedures.*

Once you've completed preparing your "DOS WORKING COPY," put the master DOS disk in a secure place. Leave the "DOS WORKING COPY" disk (from now on I'll call it the DOS disk) in the A: drive.

> *REMINDER... The same precaution regarding FORMAT applies to DISKCOPY. Be cautious. You can easily destroy important files. Check the target disk before proceeding.*

You're now armed with four ready-to-use disks, one of which is a hard disk. Three of these will boot the computer. Do you know which one won't?

# COPY FILES

Four For The Price Of One

This chapter covers several commands simultaneously. Does that mean it's jammed with jargon to learn? No. Actually, if you learn the parameters for one command, you collectively learn those for three others. That's four commands for the price of one!

The pivotal command is COPY. The bargain three are DIR, RENAME (REN), and ERASE (DEL). True, you've already used DIR in Chapters Seven and Eight. Now, though, you'll learn several power features and functional shortcuts that it shares with the others.

DON'T SKIP THROUGH THIS CHAPTER. Try *all* the examples at least once, and try them *in order*. The progression will help you *understand* important relationships. Understanding is preferable to remembering. With understanding, you can readily reconstruct what you forget.

The COPY Command

The COPY command differs from the DISKCOPY command (Chapter Eight) in that...

COPY	DISKCOPY
Copies only files.	Copies all contents of a disk.
Copies files into available space.	Wipes out anything on the target disk.
Copies only onto formatted disks.	Formats blank disks.

Try out the COPY command by copying a file from the DOS disk in the A: drive onto the hard disk. If you're picking up where you left off in the previous chapter, your DOS disk is in place. Type **COPY A:SYS.COM C:**, and press the [ENTER] key...

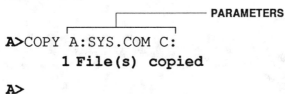

A>COPY A:SYS.COM C:
     1 File(s) copied

A> _

This time you used three parameters, two drive specifiers and one filename. You also put spaces in the proper places. Each is a serious parameter matter.

Parameter Priority

The priority of the parameters is *source* to *target*. It parallels the order in which DOS executes operations. For example, you just instructed DOS to copy a file *from* the disk in the A: drive *onto* the disk in the C: drive.

To copy in the opposite direction, type **COPY C:SYS.COM A:**, and press the [ENTER] key...

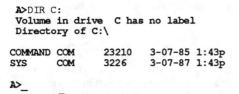

        COPY C:SYS.COM A:
 • SPACE ⌐⌐
 • SPACE ⌐⌐⌐⌐⌐⌐⌐⌐⌐

This copies the same file *from* the hard disk *to* the floppy disk in the A: drive. The priority is from and to, and goes left to right, just like you read.

Look at the directory of the hard disk to see if the copy arrived by typing **DIR C:**, and pressing the [ENTER] key...

```
A>DIR C:
Volume in drive  C has no label
Directory of C:\

COMMAND  COM     23210    3-07-85 1:43p
SYS      COM      3226    3-07-87 1:43p

A>_
```

> NOTE: *The details of your directory may differ slightly from the illustrations. The differences don't affect these examples.*

Okay. Copying one file either way is easy. Sometimes, though, it's necessary to copy a *long* list of files. This could entail tedious typing if it weren't for WILD CARDS.

Wild Card Characters

DOS provides two "wild card" characters that can represent any or all characters of filenames and extensions. These wild cards are the * (asterisk) and the ? (question mark).

The * (asterisk) can represent up to all eight filename characters, or up to three extension characters. For example, one * (asterisk) before and another after a period represent all the files on a disk. The first asterisk represents all the filenames, the second all the extensions.

With that in mind, here's how to copy all the files from the DOS disk onto the hard disk with one command. Make sure the disk in the A: drive is the DOS disk, and type **COPY A:*.* C:**...

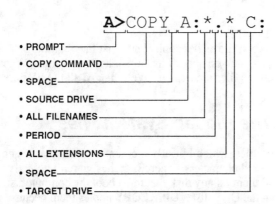

```
A>COPY A:*.* C:
```
- PROMPT
- COPY COMMAND
- SPACE
- SOURCE DRIVE
- ALL FILENAMES
- PERIOD
- ALL EXTENSIONS
- SPACE
- TARGET DRIVE

Then, watch the screen as you press the [**ENTER**] key...

```
A>COPY A:*.* C:
A:ASSIGN.COM
A:ATTRIB.EXE
A:BACKUP.COM
A:BASIC.COM
A:BASICA.COM
A:CHKDSK.COM
A:COMMAND.COM
A:COMP.COM
A:DISKCOMP.COM
A:DISKCOPY.COM
A:EDLIN.COM
A:FDISK.COM
A:FIND.EXE
A:FORMAT.COM
A:GRAPHICS.COM
A:MODE.COM
A:MORE.COM
A:PRINT.COM
A:RECOVER.COM
A:RESTORE.COM
A:SORT.EXE
A:SYS.COM
A:TREE.COM
        23 File(s) copied

A>_
```

Note how DOS lists each file as it's copied, and that the warning lights on the drives alternately switch on and off as DOS reads and writes. When the prompt reappears, all the files are copied. Well, *almost* all the files are copied.

The Hidden System Files

The "hidden" system files, which I briefly mentioned in Chapter Eight, aren't affected by the wild card characters. Therefore, they weren't copied onto the hard disk. You need them on any disk that must boot the computer, so they must be copied from the DOS disk. DISKCOPY copies them because it copies everything. The /S parameter with the FORMAT command copies them, too. Both commands however, erase all other files from the target disk. The COPY command won't copy them at all, but there is another way.

The SYS Command

The SYS (SYStem transfer) command is a single purpose variation of the COPY command. Not only is it a way to copy *just* the hidden system files from the DOS disk to another disk, it's the *only* way.

Just to see how it works, "transfer the system" to the hard disk. With the DOS disk in the A: drive, type **SYS C:**, and press the [ENTER] key...

```
A>SYS C:

System transferred

A> _
```

If you get the message No room for system on destination disk, that's okay because this is practice. Just continue.

Once the hidden system files are transferred, copy the visible COMMAND.COM file onto the C: drive. Type **COPY A:COMMAND.COM C:**, and press the [ENTER] key...

```
A>COPY A:COMMAND.COM C:
       1 File(s) copied

A> _
```

This file is already there, too. But this exercise is to reinforce the fact that both the COMMAND.COM and system files are necessary for booting.

Alternative Booting

As long as we're on the subject of ways of booting, I may as well mention that sometimes a software manufacturer will require that you boot with a particular PROGRAM DISK...

PROGRAM DISK... *the disk of an application program, such as a word processor, spreadsheet, game, etc. This disk contains the main commands, instructions, and files to run the application.*

You can boot a computer with any disk that contains the COMMAND.COM and hidden system files. But, because some newer computer systems with hard disks have special requirements, it's unwise to boot from an application program disk. The best policy is to always boot from your hard disk once your system is completely set up.

The Wild Card Filter

You already know that asterisks can be substituted for all the filenames and extensions in a directory. Now see how it can represent parts of filenames or extensions. Begin by typing **COPY A:*.EXE C:**, and pressing the [ENTER] key...

```
                    ┌──COMMMAND
                    │  ┌─SOURCE DRIVE SPECIFIER
                    │  │  ┌─WILD CARD
                    │  │  │  ┌──SPECIFIED EXTENSION
                    │  │  │  │  ┌──TARGET DRIVE SPECIFIER
     A>COPY A:*.EXE C:

     A:ATTRIB.EXE
     A:FIND.EXE
     A:JOIN.EXE
     A:SHARE.EXE
     A:SORT.EXE
     A:SUBST.EXE
             6 File(s) copied

     A> _
```

As you can see, the *only* files that copied were those with an EXE extension. This is an example of using a wild card to FILTER...

FILTER (verb)... *to select and collect, by specifying certain criteria, some but not all elements from a group.*

In the example, you filtered files ending in EXE by specifying ending with EXE in the parameter. Those with other extensions were ignored by DOS.

Now, filter all filenames beginning with the characters KEY. Type **COPY A:KEY*.* C:**...

```
          A>COPY A:KEY*.* C:

  • ALL FILENAMES ────────────┘
    BEGINNING WITH KEY

  • ALL EXTENSIONS ─────────────────┘
```

Press the [ENTER] key...

```
     KEYBDV.EXE
     KEYBFR.EXE
     KEYBUK.EXE
     KEYBGR.EXE
     KEYBIT.EXE
     KEYBSP.EXE
             6 File(s) copied

     A> _
```

These are the files that were filtered from my DOS disk. Yours may differ slightly. The point is to see how the * can substitute for any *group* of characters in a filename or extension. For substituting a *single* character in a filename or extension, there's a second wild card.

The Second Wild Card

The second wild card character, the *?* (question mark), replaces a *single* character. For example, if you want to copy only the DISKCOMP.COM and DISKCOPY.COM files, type **COPY A:DISKCO??.* C:**...

A>COPY A:DISKCO??.* C:

- **TWO CHARACTERS IN THE FILENAME**
- **ALL CHARACTERS IN THE EXTENSION**

Press the [ENTER] key...

```
A>COPY A:DISKCO??.* C:
A:DISKCOMP.COM
A:DISKCOPY.COM
         2 File(s) copied

A> _
```

The *?* wild cards are for filtering filenames and extensions having one or more letters in common. The *?* is specific, the * is general. Of course, if you use too many specifics, you can end up general. The next several examples will show you how careless use of the *?* can turn up unwanted, even unexpected, filenames. Type **COPY A:M??E.??? C:**...

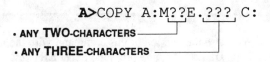

A>COPY A:M??E.??? C:

- **ANY TWO-CHARACTERS**
- **ANY THREE-CHARACTERS**

Press the [ENTER] key.....

```
A:MODE.COM
A:MORE.COM
         2 File(s) copied

A> _
```

Next, type **COPY A:???E.??? C:**, and press the **[ENTER]** key...

```
A>COPY A:???E.??? C:
A:MODE.COM
A:MORE.COM
A:TREE.COM
        3 File(s) copied

A> _
```

You picked up one more file. Change the combination by typing **COPY A:?O??.??? C:**, and pressing the **[ENTER]** key...

```
A>COPY A:?O??.??? C:
A:COMP.COM
A:JOIN.EXE
A:MODE.COM
A:MORE.COM
A:SORT.EXE
        5 File(s) copied

A> _
```

More files appear as you become less specific. If there were files named DOGS.EAT and MOON.COW on your source disk, they'd be on the list, too.

Wild DIR and DEL Commands

Wild card characters work with the DIR (DIRectory) and the ERASE, or DEL (DELete), commands. With these commands, you can affect groups of files simultaneously, or you can affect them all.

> ### UNDERSCORING THE OBVIOUS
> *When you ERASE, or DEL, one or more files, that's it! The data's gone.*

Type **ERASE C:*.*** — No. Use the version of this command with the least number of keystrokes. Type **DEL C:*.***, and press the **[ENTER]** key...

```
A>DEL C:*.*
Are you sure (Y/N)?

A> _
```

Ah. A last chance warning. The finality of this sweeping command provokes DOS to issue a warning. This time, heed the warning by typing **N**, and pressing the **[ENTER]** key which takes you safely back to the system prompt with no harm done.

Comforting? Well, unfortunately, DOS gives this last chance warning for "all files" only. For any selection other than "all files," DOS gives no warning.

UNERASE

There are software programs available that can conditionally UNERASE files. (Unerase is one computerese term that makes sense.)

How can something that's been erased still be there to be unerased? Because DOS doesn't actually erase a file. DEL, or ERASE, only modifies the filename in the directory so DOS doesn't see it.

If a filename doesn't appear in a directory, DOS treats its location as available territory. Any new files written onto the disk will record over the "erased" file.

Overwriting Files

When DOS writes data onto data, it's called overwriting. Sometimes you want to overwrite files, sometimes it's the last thing you want to do. To avoid accidentally overwriting important files, be sure you understand how DOS overwrites.

As you now know, copying a file from one disk, or directory, to another is easy. You simply enter the COPY command, then the source drive and filename followed by the target drive.

Look what happens, however, when you ignore the drive specifying parameters. Type **COPY COMMAND.COM**, and press the **[ENTER]** key...

```
A>COPY COMMAND.COM
File cannot be copied onto itself
    0 File(s) copied

A> _
```

DOS won't copy a file onto itself. That's true. It won't. But this is an ambiguous rule. More correct would be: A file cannot be copied onto itself *in the same directory — and keep its name*!

The first part of the supplement to the rule — *in the same directory* — is critical. You see, a file *can* be copied onto itself in *another* directory. You've done it in previous examples. Take a look at the directories of both drives, though, and you'll see no duplicate files. Each time you copied, the source file replaced the target file through a process called overwrite — new data replaces old.

Even though DOS won't overwrite a file in the same directory, it will in different directories. That is, one file will overwrite another when both have the same name.

Which brings us to the second part of the supplement to the rule — *and keep its name*. DOS pays attention only to the name of the file, not its contents.

Before using the COPY command, always take the precaution to check the filenames on the target disk with the DIR command. Watch for similar file-names, too. They can be confused, entered in error, then accidentally overwritten. A bad file can overwrite a good file.

If you have two different files with the same name, and want both in the same directory, rename one of them.

The RENAME Command

The RENAME, or REN, command does just what it says, and that's all. It renames a file. Try it now to get the idea. First log to the C: drive. You know how to do that, so I won't bore you with the details. Then, type **REN C:COMMAND.COM CLARK**, and press the [ENTER] key...

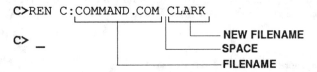

```
C>REN C:COMMAND.COM CLARK

C> _
```
NEW FILENAME
SPACE
FILENAME

Did anything happen? (Be careful. I'm going to get tricky!) Look at the directory of the C: drive. Is the COMMAND.COM file still there? Yes. It simply has a new name—Clark.

Rename it again, this time use drive specifying paramaters to change its location. Type **REN C:CLARK A:SUPERMAN**, and press the [ENTER] key...

```
C>REN C:CLARK A:SUPERMAN
Invalid parameter

C> _
```

As you can see, something didn't work. (I told you I was going to get tricky.) DOS rejected the command, and generated the error message, *Invalid parameter.* CLARK didn't change to SUPERMAN. But even SUPERMAN could not have moved from the C: drive to the A: drive, anyway. (Use the DIR command to check the C: drive to make sure.) As I told you at the outset, DOS limits REN to changing a file's name only. It can't change the location of a file.

> *NOTE: If you're using some version of DOS earlier than 3.1, the error message won't appear, and the file's name will change. The file's location never changes.*

Renaming With COPY

If, for some reason, you want more than one copy of the same file in a directory, DOS provides the means to *rename as you copy.* It's a one step process. For example, type **COPY C:CLARK C:SUPERMAN**, and press the [ENTER] key...

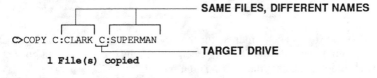

```
                                    ——————— SAME FILES, DIFFERENT NAMES
           ┌──────────┬──────────┐
C>COPY C:CLARK C:SUPERMAN
           └──┘       └──┘    ——————— TARGET DRIVE
     1 File(s) copied

C> _
```

Simultaneously, DOS copies *and* changes the name of a file. Now there are two identical COMMAND.COM files on the C: drive, both CLARK and SUPERMAN. Despite the name changes, each is the COMMAND.COM file–with a new name.

What about different directories? Copying and renaming a file from one directory to another depends simply on appropriate drive specifying parameters. But you knew that was the answer, didn't you?

> *AVOID ACCIDENTALLY OVERWRITING FILES*
> *Before using the COPY command, use the DIR command to check the filenames on the target disk.*
> *Check spelling, too. Similar spelling of files can be risky.*

SOME COPY COMMAND SPECIALTIES

The Devices

The COPY command can also be used in connection with a DEVICE...

DEVICE... computerese for hardware such as keyboard, monitor, or printer. It's a synonym of another computerese term: PERIPHERAL.

You can use a device, by name, just as you would a filename. Here are the principle devices and their names...

Devices	*Ports for Devices*
Keyboard & Screen	*CON*
Printers	*LPT1 (PRN), LPT2, & LPT3*
Modem, Mouse, etc.	*COM1 (AUX) & COM2*

CON (CONsole) is computerese for the keyboard and screen. The keyboard is an input device, the display, or screen, shows the output. If data goes no further than the screen, the screen *is* the output.

Now, we're going to directly interface (I use this word every chance I get) with the disk operating system.

Remove the write protection from the DOS working disk. You'll restore it after these exercises. Put it into the A: drive and close it's door.

COPY From CON

Here's how to make a text file (that's a file full of text) by copying from the CON, and outputting (computerese, but recognizable) it to a disk.

First, clear your screen of everything except the system prompt. Type **CLS** (CLear Screen), and press the [ENTER] key.

Log onto the A: drive, then tell DOS to "COPY from the CONsole a file called SCROLL.TXT" by typing **COPY CON SCROLL.TXT**, and pressing the [ENTER] key...

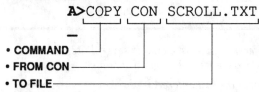

A>COPY CON SCROLL.TXT

• COMMAND
• FROM CON
• TO FILE

DOS reads instructions progressively from left to right. Because you entered CON *before* the name of the file, DOS knows to copy *from* CON.

Next, put some text into the file by typing the sentence **THIS IS A LINE**...

```
A>COPY CON SCROLL.TXT
THIS IS A LINE_
```

Press the [ENTER] key...

```
A>COPY CON SCROLL.TXT
THIS IS A LINE

_
```

Now the easy way to type, press the **F3** key...

```
A>COPY CON SCROLL.TXT
THIS IS A LINE
THIS IS A LINE_
```

How about that?! The **F3** key retypes THIS IS A LINE. Press the [ENTER] key and the **F3** key again to get to the next line.

Press the **F3** and [ENTER] keys at least thirty more times. Yes, that's right, THIRTY TIMES.

Finally, end the file. Press the **F6** key (or press the [CTRL] key while typing **Z**), followed by the [ENTER] key...

```
THIS IS A LINE
THIS IS A LINE
THIS IS A LINE
THIS IS A LINE
THIS IS A LINE
^Z
     1 File(s) copied

A> _
```

The **F6** key, or **^Z**, means "end of file." Pressing the **[ENTER]** key this time causes DOS to copy the text lines from the CON onto the disk in the logged drive, creating a file, and naming it SCROLL.TXT!

Check to see if the file's there with the DIR command. Then check to see if the contents are there. How? The COPY command again.

> *Your DOS reference manual explains several uses for the function keys. You learned two in this chapter*
>
> *F3 means repeat the last entered keystrokes.*
>
> *F6, which is the same as holding down the [CTRL] and pressing the Z key, means "end of file" (typing the ^ and Z keys won't work!).*

COPY To CON

The best way to look inside a text file is with a word processor. But a quick and easy way to peek inside a text file, is COPY to CON. Use this method now to take a peek inside the SCROLL.TXT file.

Begin at the system prompt. Type **COPY A:SCROLL.TXT CON:**, and press the **[ENTER]** key...

```
A>COPY A:SCROLL.TXT CON
THIS IS A LINE
THIS IS A LINE
THIS IS A LINE
THIS IS A LINE
THIS IS A LINE
THIS IS A LINE

THIS IS A LINE
THIS IS A LINE
THIS IS A LINE
THIS IS A LINE
THIS IS A LINE
THIS IS A LINE

     1 File(s) copied

A>_
```

Because you entered CON *after* the name of the file, DOS knows to copy *to* CON. DOS reads the instructions as "copy the SCROLL.TXT file onto the screen," and responds obediently.

NOTE: The SCROLL.TXT file is longer than twenty-four lines, so it scrolls by before you can read it. You can stop and start scrolling with the [CTRL] S command. This is explained in Chapter Seven, page 33 of Easy DOS It!

Besides helping you take quick peeks when looking for some particular information, this technique is the simplest way to solve the recurring "Mystery of the Cryptic Filename." When the name of a file doesn't give a clue to its content, you COPY it to CON, and see what's what!

REMINDER... Match the parameter order to the result you want.

COPY CON FILENAME... means copy from CON to a file with a specified name

COPY FILENAME CON... means copy a specified file onto the CON

COPY to PRN

This is the third, and last, special way to use the COPY command. This time, you print the file from the disk.

Make sure your printer's on, then type **COPY A:SCROLL.TXT PRN**, and press the **[ENTER]** key...

```
A>COPY A:SCROLL.TXT PRN
        1 File(s) copied

A> _
```

This is one way that DOS will print a file. In this case, the printer port was called PRN...

PRN... means default printer port. When your computer system is set up, the PRN is usually the LPT1 port. LPT1 means Line PrinTer 1. DOS supports three line, commonly called parallel, printers. Alternatives are LPT2 or LPT3 depending on your system's configuration. (Serial printers use the COM1 or COM2 ports.)

By the way, don't expect classy formatting (margins, tabs, bold type, underlining, etc.) when copying from a file to a device, either CON or PRN. For text to be presentable, it must be processed with an application program such as a word processor.

Clean Up Before Leaving This Chapter

Before moving onto the next chapter, get rid of the files you copied onto the hard disk by typing, from either prompt, **DEL C:*.***, and press the **[ENTER]** key...

```
A>DEL C:*.*
Are you sure (Y/N)?

A> _
```

You saw this last chance warning before. This time, delete all the files. Type **Y**, and press the **[ENTER]** key...

Not much seems to happen. DOS just does its duty without comment.

Now all but the hidden system files are gone. So, in order that you may boot from the C: drive, copy the COMMAND.COM file from the DOS disk. (C'mon, you know how to do it!)

Remember to restore write protection to the DOS disk.

Finally...

So ends this long chapter. If you wearied along the way, take comfort in the fact that, while learning the COPY command, you also learned some subtleties of the DIR, REN, and ERASE (DEL) commands. You discovered the SYS command, too. That's FIVE for the price of ONE. You got one more than promised.

As you use DOS, you'll discover interesting variations. For example, there are several other useful ways to use the COPY command. Don't worry about them now, though. Trying to learn everything about DOS is a sure way to become confused. Then you'll blame DOS for being hard to learn. As you have seen, it's easy.

HARD DISK DIRECTORIES

So What Do You Know So Far?

Let's see. There are three assumptions most people make about a hard disk by now...

1. It's a bigger disk than a floppy disk.
2. It's a disk sealed in a box.
3. It's hard to use.

The first two assumptions are correct. A hard disk is at least ten times bigger than a floppy disk, and it is sealed in a box about the same size as a floppy disk drive.

The problem with these two correct assumptions is they seem to conflict. And, I'll be the first to admit that verifying them can be a temptation. How is it that one of two similar size boxes can contain ten or more times the other's volume? Those endowed with excessive curiosity may yearn to tamper with the seal of a hard disk to find out.

Well, it's not necessary to break into your hard disk. The secret's revealed in the Appendix. If you're one of the curious, you already referred to it. The hard disk is actually an assembly of several disks — also called platters. The design is more efficient for data storage than the floppy disk and drive combination. That's all there is to it.

The third assumption, that a hard disk is hard to use, is not correct. A hard disk is not hard to use. Although, there are several ways taught that make it seem a technical terror. But, this book doesn't teach those ways. You'll have to find out how to make a hard disk hard to use elsewhere.

The Big Bin

A newly formatted hard disk can be likened to a big, empty bin. Imagine such a container into which you've pitched months of written memos, notes, reports, chapters, outlines, and other materials, in no particular order. True, you were shrewd enough to have put every one of those records into

individual folders. You labelled them, too, with unique code names, most of which you forgot in a few days. And now it's time to find a specific document in that mass of miscellany.

Revolting state to contemplate, isn't it? Nevertheless, it's a reasonable representation of the fate of anyone using a hard disk without some clearly defined method of organization.

It Begins With One

Whenever you format a disk, DOS makes a main directory called the ROOT...

> **ROOT**... the main directory of every formatted disk.

The root directory contains technical information such as: the LABEL of the disk, the DATE CREATED, the TIME CREATED, any ATTRIBUTES, the FAT (File Allocation Tables), and the disk's size in bytes. Wait. Don't do it. Don't stop reading just to memorize this technical information. It's unlikely you'll ever need to know those details. I was just computerese dropping.

The important thing to remember is that DOS makes the root directory. DOS also provides the means (relevant commands and computerese to be explained in the next chapter) for you to make and manipulate directories of your own. Such a person-made directory is called a SUBDIRECTORY...

> **SUBDIRECTORY**... a file that contains directory entries, but can be used like any disk directory including the root.

You can make as many subdirectories in a hard disk as you like. There's no limit to the number other than disk space. And, since a subdirectory can be used like any directory including the root, you can make subdirectories in subdirectories.

Again I'll remind you that a hard disk has only one directory — the root — until you add others — the subdirectories. So, any hard disk that's hard to use because it contains too many subdirectories can't be blamed on DOS.

NOTE: Technically, all directories are subdirectories of the root directory. The terms directory and subdirectory are interchangeably used throughout the computer industry, including this book.

The Filing Cabinet Metaphor

In Chapter Two, I used file folders as metaphorical equivalents of those discrete groups of stored data called files. In Chapter Seven, I extended this metaphor to cover groups of files on a floppy disk — a file drawer. Then, in Chapter Eight, in the Appendix, even at the beginning of this chapter, I contrasted the relative capacities of hard and floppy disks, the former having an enormous superiority in size. Throughout, I neglected to favor you with another metaphor! Tsk, tsk. I'll take care of that oversight now with — the filing cabinet metaphor.

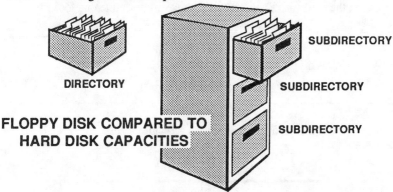

DIRECTORY

SUBDIRECTORY

SUBDIRECTORY

FLOPPY DISK COMPARED TO HARD DISK CAPACITIES

SUBDIRECTORY

A file drawer, the metaphor for a floppy disk, can hold fewer files than a filing cabinet, the metaphor for a hard disk. Even better, its several drawers makes it a reasonable metaphorical match to a hard disk containing several subdirectories.

On The Levels

Another reason such a filing system is a good metaphor for directory disposition is because both are organized in a HIERARCHY...

> **HIERARCHY**... *any subject or group organized or classified into successive ranks or grades with each level subordinate to the one above.*

The hierarchy is the basis of DOS directory organization. The most familiar hierarchy is "the family tree" from which we trace our "roots." A severely simple family tree looks like this...

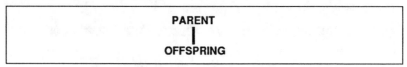

A family tree hierarchy traces the lineage to and from the source, or parent. It shows who's derived from whom...

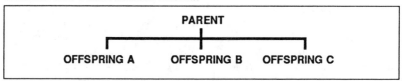

A DOS hierarchy works much the same way, except the parent is the root directory; the offspring a subdirectory. A severely simple one looks like this...

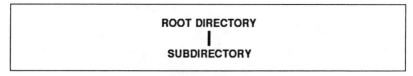

As more subdirectories appear, a familiar structure forms...

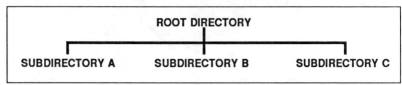

It looks even more familiar this way...

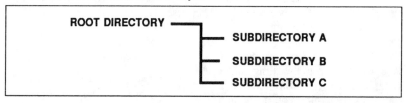

Recognize it? It's an OUTLINE. A hierarchy, in diagram form, is called an outline.

If you understand outlining, hierarchies are simple. If, however, you're like most people, you never took to outlining in school. All those Roman numerals, upper and lower case letters, and brackets were easier to use in retrospect. In other words, the easy way was to write a report or an essay, then make an outline. Too bad if that's the way you approached outlining because it's the easiest way to organize the elements of just about any subject. It's no more complicated than a shopping list. It definitely saves enormous amounts of time. Besides all that, you need outlining for organizing subdirectories. Aren't you sorry you didn't work harder in school? Here's an example with more than one level of subdirectories...

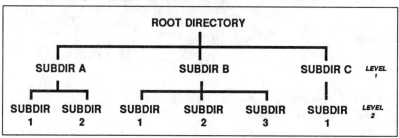

There are two levels of subdirectories shown here. Or, if you want to start counting from the root, there are three levels of directories. Neither counting method is official as far as I know. The point is, a subdirectory within a subdirectory is considered the next level down.

Don't worry if outlines and hierarchies are a little hazy. The concepts are easy to pick up once you've got the main idea.

What's a Nice Tree Like You Doing In a Filing Cabinet?

A hierarchy is sometimes referred to as a "tree structure." In DOS, it's *always* referred to that way. Actually, in DOS, it's referred to as an upside down tree structure — because the root's on top!

But, the terms "up" and "down" and "higher levels" and "lower levels" only make sense if the tree is upside down because the root is always referred to as the "top" of the hierarchy.

The idea of a root directory doesn't seem to conform to the filing cabinet metaphor, does it? Admittedly, a root isn't something you'd find in a typical file drawer. A root is more likely something you'd associate with a tree. In DOS, there seems to be no way to avoid putting files and directories into roots and trees!

Over the years, more metaphors appear. Although they're attempts to clarify multiple directories, the awkward lack of unity has complicated rather than clarified the subject. The contradictions can't be completely avoided (I've tried) because many are built into the DOS commands.

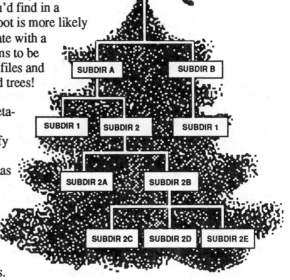

It seems that the only element interminably hard about hard disks is the necessity to submit to computerese.

It may be easier to ignore the pictures of upside down trees and filing cabinets, and focus on hierarchies for what they are — outlines in diagram form.

Are You Ready For a Hard Disk?

You may be wondering, and I don't blame you, about the rationale for learning the principles of organizing large numbers of files *before* learning to use the hard disk. Because it's easier to learn the compulsory commands and computerese for hard disks if you know *why* you're learning them. That's my opinion, and I'm sticking to it.

11 *SUBDIRECTORY COMMANDS*

NOTE: THE PROCEDURES IN THIS CHAPTER ARE
BASED ON USING A BLANK, FORMATTED WITH
SYSTEM HARD DISK AS DESCRIBED IN CHAPTER
EIGHT AND THE APPENDIX.

IF YOU HAVE FILES ON YOUR HARD DISK, THE PRO-
CEDURES WILL STILL WORK, BUT THE ILLUSTRA-
TIONS WON'T MATCH YOUR SCREEN.

Some Hard Words

Fortunately, DOS favors us with easy-to-learn commands to make, change,
and remove subdirectories. UNfortunately, learning some of the jargon
(Yes, I mean computerese!) that goes with them can be perplexing.

The following exercise is designed to make your first experience with these
commands as painless as possible. It will help you establish a basic
understanding of subdirectories.

After the exercise, the rest of the chapter helps you analyze your results.
So, don't skip or just read it over. Do the entire exercise on a computer.

An Interactive Exercise

BEFORE PROCEEDING...

*In the following exercise, you use the backslash (\) key.
The backslash is one of those keys found only on computer
keyboards. Typewriters don't have it.*

1. Begin at the system prompt of the C: drive. If you're not there, type **C:**
   at whatever prompt is on the screen, and press the [ENTER] key...

   ?>C:

   ◻ _

2. Type **CD**, and press the [ENTER] key...

   ◻CD
   C:\ ——————————— THIS SHOULD BE
                       YOUR RESULT
   ◻_

   *NOTE: If not, type CD\, and press the [ENTER] key, and
   try again. If you get the **Invalid parameter** message after
   pressing the [ENTER] key, you probably typed the /
   (slash) key instead of the \ (backslash) key. Try again.*

3. Type **MD STOOGES**, and press the [ENTER] key...

   ◻MD STOOGES

   ◻ _

4. Type **CD STOOGES**, and press the [ENTER] key...

   ◻CD STOOGES

   ◻ _

5. Type **DIR**, and press the **[ENTER]** key...

```
C>DIR

Volume in drive C has no label
Directory of C:\STOOGES

  .           <DIR>   5-5-87   13:22
  ..          <DIR>   5-5-87   13:22
    2 File(s)   xxxxxxxx bytes free
```

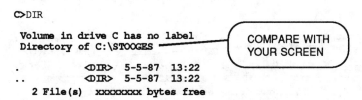

COMPARE WITH
YOUR SCREEN

6. Type **MD LARRY**, and press the **[ENTER]** key...

```
C>MD LARRY

C> _
```

7. Type **MD MOE**, and press the **[ENTER]** key...

```
C>MD MOE

C> _
```

8. Type **MD CURLEY**, and press the **[ENTER]** key...

```
C>MD CURLEY

C> _
```

9. Type **DIR**, and press the **[ENTER]** key...

```
C>DIR

Volume in drive C has no label
Directory of C:\STOOGES

  .           <DIR>   5-5-87   13:22
  ..          <DIR>   5-5-87   13:22
LARRY         <DIR>   5-5-87   13:22
MOE           <DIR>   5-5-87   13:22
CURLEY        <DIR>   5-5-87   13:22
    5 File(s)   xxxxxxxx bytes free
```

COMPARE WITH
YOUR SCREEN

10. Type **CD ..** (The dots are periods!), and press the **[ENTER]** key...

```
C>CD ..

C> _
```

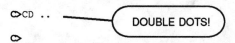

DOUBLE DOTS!

11. Type **DIR**, and press the [ENTER] key...

```
C>DIR

Volume in drive C has no label
Directory of C:\

STOOGES        <DIR>     5-5-87  13:22
COMMAND   COM   23210    5-5-87  13:22
    2 File(s)   xxxxxxxx bytes free
```

COMPARE WITH YOUR SCREEN

12. Type **CD STOOGES**, and press the [ENTER] key...

```
C>CD STOOGES

C> _
```

13. Type **DIR**, and press the [ENTER] key...

```
C>DIR

Volume in drive C has no label
Directory of C:\STOOGES

.          <DIR>   5-5-87   13:22
..         <DIR>   5-5-87   13:22
LARRY      <DIR>   5-5-87   13:22
MOE        <DIR>   5-5-87   13:22
CURLEY     <DIR>   5-5-87   13:22
    5 File(s)   xxxxxxxx bytes free
```

COMPARE WITH YOUR SCREEN

14. Type **CD MOE**, and press the [ENTER] key...

```
C>CD MOE

C> _
```

15. Type **DIR**, and press the [ENTER] key...

```
C>DIR

Volume in drive C has no label
Directory of C:\STOOGES\MOE

.          <DIR>   5-5-87   13:22
..         <DIR>   5-5-87   13:22
    2 File(s)   xxxxxxxx bytes free
```

COMPARE WITH YOUR SCREEN

16. Type **CD **, and press the [ENTER] key...

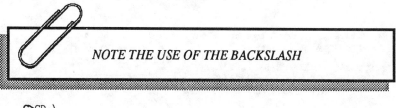

NOTE THE USE OF THE BACKSLASH

```
C>CD \
C> _
```

17. Type **DIR**, and press the [ENTER] key...

```
C>DIR

Volume in drive C has no label
Directory of C:\

STOOGES        <DIR>    5-5-87  13:22
COMMAND   COM   23210   5-5-87  13:22
        2 File(s)   xxxxxxxx bytes free
```

COMPARE WITH
YOUR SCREEN

18. Type **CD \\STOOGES\\CURLEY**, and press the [ENTER] key...

```
C>CD \STOOGES\CURLEY

C> _
```

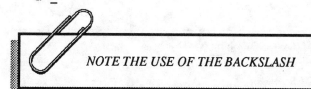

NOTE THE USE OF THE BACKSLASH

19. Type **DIR**, and press the [ENTER] key...

```
C>DIR

Volume in drive C has no label
Directory of C:\STOOGES\CURLEY

.           <DIR>  5-5-87  13:22
..          <DIR>  5-5-87  13:22
    2 File(s)   xxxxxxxx bytes free
```

COMPARE WITH
YOUR SCREEN

20. Type **CD **, and press the [ENTER] key...

```
C>CD \

C> _
```

21. Type **DIR**, and press the **[ENTER]** key...

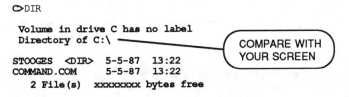

```
C>DIR

Volume in drive C has no label
Directory of C:\

STOOGES   <DIR>   5-5-87   13:22
COMMAND.COM       5-5-87   13:22
    2 File(s)   xxxxxxxx bytes free
```

COMPARE WITH
YOUR SCREEN

That's it. End of exercise. Did you go through it all on a computer? I hope so. It will do little good for you to just read it, or, worse, skip it. The imperative here is to experience those operations outlined in the exercise *as given*. So, let's assume you successfully completed the exercise.

What HAVE You Done?

For one thing, you made your hard disk into a do-it-yourself training disk as you marked off and named several directories. While you were at it, you ran almost all the commands you'll probably ever need for using a hard disk. The hierarchy of your results should look like this...

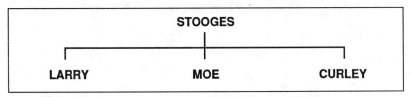

Here's the outline version of the same results...

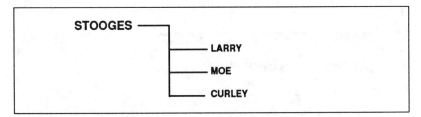

The Backslash Command?

You couldn't help but notice the big deal I made of the backslash (\) character in the exercise. Understanding the backslash is fundamental to understanding hard disk file organization. It's so important, I've conferred upon it the designation of DOS command. That's why it's listed under the Additional Eight hard disk commands in Chapter Fourteen.

The reason I consider the backslash character so important is because it's the major stumbling block met by those learning to use hard disks.

How can one little character be so harmful? Because it has two meanings! Yes, *two* meanings which aren't the same, but are often used *at the same time*! You've been duly alerted, so here we go.

The First Backslash Meaning

Look at any directory of any formatted disk, floppy or hard. You see a \ following the drive designator. For example, the directory of a blank, formatted disk looks like this...

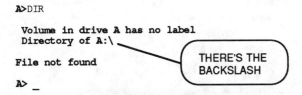

```
A>DIR

  Volume in drive A has no label
  Directory of A:\

File not found                    THERE'S THE
                                  BACKSLASH
A> _
```

The reason you always see the \ is because, as you recall from the previous chapter, during the FORMAT procedure, DOS automatically creates the root directory. The \ means root directory. That's the first meaning of this symbol. Easy enough. Right?

The Second Backslash Meaning

Except for the root directory, all other directories, the subdirectories, are one or more levels down. That's why they're called subdirectories. DOS finds a subdirectory by following a PATH...

> **PATH...** *the route to a subdirectory, or to a file in a subdirectory.*

Here's a diagram showing a clearly marked path to one subdirectory on your hard disk...

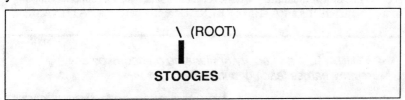

\ (ROOT)

STOOGES

DOS needs directions to find this subdirectory, just as we require a diagram to show us the way. DOS, however, demands directions in a specific format. The backslashes provide the nexus (Take a break, and look it up!) to the format. In plain words, this diagram means "the path is from the root directory to the STOOGES subdirectory." But in DOS talk, it looks like this...

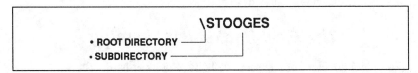

The root directory can contain one or more subdirectories. So can a subdirectory. Here's a diagram showing the STOOGES subdirectory with three familiar subdirectories...

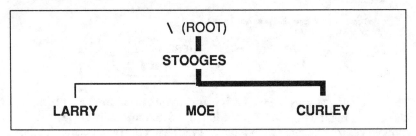

The bold line in the diagram, which begins at the root directory, goes through the STOOGES subdirectory, and ends at the CURLEY subdirectory, is marking a path to *one* subdirectory. In DOS talk, it looks like this...

\STOOGES\CURLEY
- ROOT DIRECTORY
- SUBDIRECTORY
- PATH MARKER
- SUBDIRECTORY

And, in plain words, it means "the path is from the root to the STOOGES subdirectory to the CURLEY subdirectory." This is an example of the second backslash meaning. Whenever a backslash is preceeded by one or more characters it's a PATHMARKER. Here it's part of a PATHNAME...

PATHNAME... a directory or filename preceded by any directory names leading to it.

Take special note that there are no spaces in a pathname. The path marker is all that separates one subdirectory from another.

Sometimes, the drive specifier is considered part of the pathname, too. For example, C:\STOOGES and C:\STOOGES\CURLEY would be the path-names in the C: drive.

Also note that the path information in a pathname always reads from left to right — drive to directory to subdirectory to next subdirectory — some-times ending in a filename.

Pathnames and Filenames

A pathname's purpose is to direct DOS to a particular directory, sometimes a file within that directory. It's a step by step process because DOS isn't sophisticated enough to go directly from the source to the target. It must take every, consecutive, incremental step.

In fact, when using more than one directory, the *only* way DOS can find a file in a subdirectory is by following a path. To find, for example, a text file about a bald head (BALD.TXT), the pathname would be...

```
          \STOOGES\CURLEY\BALD.TXT
• ROOT DIRECTORY ─┘
• DIRECTORY ───────────┘
• PATH MARKER ──────────────┘
• SUBDIRECTORY ──────────────────┘
• PATH MARKER ─────────────────────────┘
• FILENAME ───────────────────────────────┘
```

A pathname goes no further than a filename, though, because a data file can't contain subdirectories.

Here are five pathnames of subdirectories you made...

Type	Pathname
• ROOT DIRECTORY ───	\
• A DIRECTORY ───────	\STOOGES
• SUBDIRECTORIES ─┬──	\STOOGES\LARRY
├──	\STOOGES\MOE
└──	\STOOGES\CURLEY

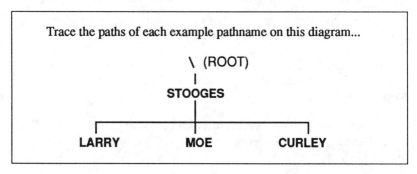

Trace the paths of each example pathname on this diagram...

\ (ROOT)
|
STOOGES
|
LARRY   MOE   CURLEY

Admit it, now. This stuff is starting to make sense, isn't it? Once you've mastered the two backslash rules, you'll discover even the most complex hard disk hierarchy is easy to decipher.

THE EASY PATHNAME RULE

Although there are yet shorter ways to specify pathnames and filenames, at this time the explanations could lead to confusion. So, until you gain experience, I recommend that you...

ALWAYS BEGIN A PATHNAME AT THE ROOT.

One more point. You know the stand-alone \ always means root directory, but is its pathname \\? No. One \ is enough. The complete pathname for the root is just one backslash.

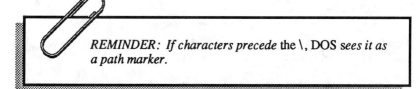

REMINDER: If characters precede the \, DOS sees it as a path marker.

? *"WHAT'S THE ONLY TREE IN THE WORLD WITH THE ROOT ON TOP?"*

(Yep. The DOS tree.)

Pathnames As Parameters

In Chapter Nine, you learned how to selectively filter a batch of files using parameters such as wild cards and switches. Pathnames can be parameters, too.

Here's an example of a pathname as a parameter. At the C: prompt, type **DIR \STOOGES**, and press the [ENTER] key...

```
C>DIR \STOOGES

    Volume in drive C has no label
    Directory of C:\STOOGES

    .          <DIR>    5-5-87   13:22
    ..         <DIR>    5-5-87   13:22
    LARRY      <DIR>    5-5-87   13:22
    MOE        <DIR>    5-5-87   13:22
    CURLEY     <DIR>    5-5-87   13:22
        5 File(s)   xxxxxxxx bytes free
```

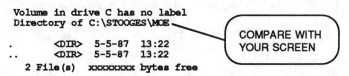

COMPARE WITH
YOUR SCREEN

The pathname parameter told DOS to show you the contents of the STOOGES directory. To look in the MOE subdirectory, type **DIR \STOOGES\MOE**, and press the [ENTER] key...

```
C>DIR \STOOGES\MOE

    Volume in drive C has no label
    Directory of C:\STOOGES\MOE

    .          <DIR>    5-5-87   13:22
    ..         <DIR>    5-5-87   13:22
        2 File(s)   xxxxxxxx bytes free
```

COMPARE WITH
YOUR SCREEN

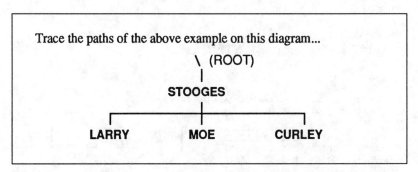

Trace the paths of the above example on this diagram...

\ (ROOT)
|
STOOGES
|
LARRY   MOE   CURLEY

When you are new to hard disk directories, remembering the pathname can be perplexing. It's not always so easy to recall pathnames, even for veteran DOS users. Fortunately, DOS offers another way.

The Change Directory Command

Although you can gain access to any directory by using pathnames as parameters, it's easier with CD, the Change Directory command.

> *In early versions of DOS, the abbreviation for the Change Directory command was CHDIR (CHange DIRectory). New versions offer CD as an alternative. I prefer CD.*

The command logs you from one directory to another. Since you're *logging*, shouldn't the new directory be called the *logged directory*? Maybe it should be called the *changed directory*. No, neither of these. DOS calls the changed, logged directory the CURRENT DIRECTORY...

> **CURRENT DIRECTORY...** the **changed, logged,** and **default** directory; the directory that responds to commands.

As you can see, the definition for the current directory is, for all practical purposes, identical to the definition for the logged, or default, drive.

Now try it. Type **CD STOOGES**, and press the **[ENTER]** key...

```
C>CD STOOGES

C> _
```

Now the default, logged, current directory is \STOOGES. Take a look by typing **DIR**, and pressing the **[ENTER]** key...

```
C>DIR

    Volume in drive C has no label
    Directory of C:\STOOGES

    .        <DIR>    5-5-87   13:22
    ..       <DIR>    5-5-87   13:22
    LARRY    <DIR>    5-5-87   13:22
    MOE      <DIR>    5-5-87   13:22
    CURLEY   <DIR>    5-5-87   13:22
       5 File(s)   xxxxxxxx bytes free
```

THE CURRENT
DIRECTORY LABEL

True, it took two steps instead of one to get here, as opposed to using the pathname as a parameter. But any additional commands can be used now without typing a pathname parameter.

What IS the Current Directory, Anyway?

Whenever you run the DIR command, the name of the current directory appears at the top. But sometimes it scrolls out of sight, and you don't notice it. Here's an easy way to determine the current directory. Type **CD**, and press the **[ENTER]** key...

```
C>CD

C:\STOOGES ———    THIS SHOULD BE
                   YOUR RESULT
```

Entering the CD command without a parameter displays both the logged drive and the current directory. CD changes the directory only if it's followed by a directory name.

> *Remember the difference...*
>
> *CD (directory name) = Change Directory to (directory name)*
>
> *CD = displays Current Directory — "Check Directory"*

?

• •

QUICKIE QUIZ

Do you remember how to log onto a drive?

Do you know the meaning of default drive?

• •

Presumably you correctly answered "yes" to both questions. So, give yourself a reward. (If you're not certain, go back to Chapter Six to refresh your memory.)

Subdirectories Are Files

It came as a shock to me to discover that a subdirectory is a file. The shock didn't last long. I'm fine now. But, the discovery made it easy for me to understand why a subdirectory must follow the DOS filename and extension rules. A subdirectory's name is limited to eight characters, and it can't have the same name as another subdirectory. Extensions are legal, but I recommend you don't bother with them. Extensions on subdirectories make subdirectory names too similar to filenames. (Rules for filenames and extensions were covered in Chapter Seven.)

The Make Directory Command

DOS makes the root directory, but you must make all subdirectories. And, even though you're making subdirectories, you use the Make Directory command! Ah, well. At least doing it is a straightforward process. You simply type the MD (make directory), followed by the subdirectory name.

> *In early versions of DOS, the abbreviation for the command was MKDIR (MaKe DIRectory). New versions offer MD as an alternative. I prefer MD.*

Just as you made several dummy directories (and I mean that in more than one way) in the exercise, now make a useful subdirectory, one to contain your DOS files. Its proper place is in the root directory. So, before making it, log onto the root directory by typing **CD **, and pressing the **[ENTER]** key...

```
C>CD \

C> _
```

A directory name should be both easy to type and as descriptive as possible. For DOS files, the obvious choice is DOS. Type **MD DOS**, the press the **[ENTER]** key...

```
C>MD DOS

C> _
```

The result doesn't provide much of a clue as to whether the MD command worked or not, does it? Take a look by typing **DIR**, and pressing the **[ENTER]** key...

```
Volume in drive C has no label
Directory of C:\

DOS            <DIR>   5-5-87  13:47
STOOGES        <DIR>   5-5-87  13:22
    2 File(s)  xxxxxxxx bytes free
```

TWO
SUBDIRECTORIES

Success! The root directory contains two subdirectories now. With the addition of this directory, the hierarchy takes on a new look...

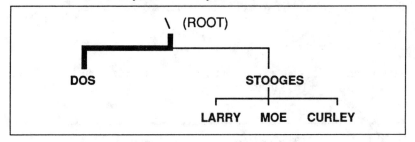

Note that I marked the path of this new subdirectory. Its pathname is \DOS.

Next, look inside \DOS. By now you know there are two ways to do it.

1. Enter DIR with the pathname as parameter.
   (DIR \DOS)

2. Enter DIR after logging onto the subdirectory.
   (CD \DOS)

Either way, the result looks like this...

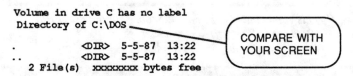

```
Volume in drive C has no label
Directory of C:\DOS
  .            <DIR>    5-5-87   13:22
  ..           <DIR>    5-5-87   13:22
     2 File(s)   xxxxxxxx bytes free
```

COMPARE WITH YOUR SCREEN

And that's all it takes to master the Make Directory command.

What's DOTS?

No doubt you noticed the .<DIR> and .. <DIR> files. They're the first two files in any directory except the root. DOS manufactures them whenever you make a directory. We'll call one SINGLE DOT, the other DOUBLE DOT.

They are reference files for DOS. The single dot describes the current directory and its location in the hierarchical tree. The double dot describes the preceding directory, the next level up in the hierarchy.

DOS uses them, so you can ignore them. Or, if you can't stand leaving them alone, use the double dot as an easy way to type a parameter. For example, with the CD command, you can change directories up one level.

The double dot can be used as generic shorthand for the previous pathname regardless of your location, unless of course you're logged to the root directory. If you're in the root directory, you'll see the message...

```
C>CD ..
Invalid directory
```

Not only are you as high as you can go, but there's never a double dot file in a root directory for DOS to use anyway!

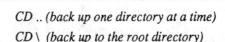

> *CD .. (back up one directory at a time)*
>
> *CD \ (back up to the root directory)*

The Remove Directory Command

When you no longer need a directory, you can remove it with the RD (Remove Directory) command. To give you some practical experience with this command, remove the directories you made during the interactive exercise. The process is easy.

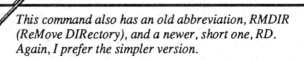

> *This command also has an old abbreviation, RMDIR (ReMove DIRectory), and a newer, short one, RD. Again, I prefer the simpler version.*

There are two conditions, though, before the RD command will work. These are built in safeguards against accidental subdirectory destruction. First, the subdirectory must be empty — no files or other subdirectories. Second, the directory to be removed can't be the current directory. You can't erase a subdirectory if you're in it.

> **THE REMOVE DIRECTORY ROUTINE**
> 1. *CD to the directory you want to remove.*
> 2. *Check current directory.*
> 3. *DEL all files in the directory.*
> 4. *CD to the root directory.*
> 5. *RD the empty directory.*
>
> *(Remember — SUBDIRECTORY and DIRECTORY are interchangeable terms.)*

You can't remove a directory that contains any files or other directories. The only files in the \STOOGES directory are three other directories. So, remove them first. Type **CD\STOOGES**, and press the [ENTER] key...

```
C>CD \STOOGES

C> _
```

Something happened. It did. Use DIR to see. There are three subdirectories, right?

Type **RD \STOOGES\LARRY**, and press the [ENTER] key. The prompt still doesn't change. Then type **RD \STOOGES\MOE**, and press the [ENTER] key. Finally, type **RD \STOOGES\CURLEY**, and press the [ENTER] key. Still the prompt remains the same. At least there are no error messages, so you must be doing something right.

If you do get a message, it'll probably be...

```
Invalid path, not directory
or directory not empty
```

This is the "generic" error message of the RD command. It's up to you to figure out which correction to make. Usually, it simply means the directory isn't empty.

Now type **DIR**, and press the [ENTER] key...

```
C>DIR

    Volume in drive C has no label
    Directory of C:\STOOGES

    .          <DIR>    5-5-87   13:22          COMPARE WITH
    ..         <DIR>    5-5-87   13:22          YOUR SCREEN
        2 File(s)   xxxxxxxx bytes free
```

See? The three subdirectories are gone. If your screen matches, type **CD ..**, and press the [ENTER] key to back up one level. This puts you into the root directory. You could also have gotten there by typing CD \, but I wanted you to try this.

The final step is to type **RD \STOOGES**, and press the [ENTER] key.

That's it. The root directory should show only one subdirectory — DOS.

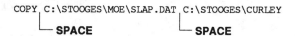

> NOTE...
> If you've been following the exercises in this book starting
> with a fresh hard disk, all that remains in the root directory
> at this point should be the COMMAND.COM file and the
> DOS subdirectory. Oh, yes. The hidden system files are
> there, too.

MORE ABOUT THE COPY COMMAND
Copying Files To and From Directories

In Chapter Nine you learned how to copy files from drive to drive. Eventually, after you've been computing a while, you'll find yourself needing to copy files from directory to directory. You may as well find out how now. Later, you'll no doubt be in a hurry.

Both procedures are basically the same. The only real difference is the additional typing needed for directory to directory copying. Admittedly, it can become complicated. For example...

```
COPY C:\STOOGES\MOE\SLAP.DAT C:\STOOGES\CURLEY
     └ SPACE              └ SPACE
```

Formidable as that amount of typing appears (there are more fearsome examples!), the process is easy to understand if you pay attention to the details. Rather than explain this example, though, I'll start you off on something more practical...

```
COPY A:*.* C:
     │    └ SPACE
     └─ SPACE
```

It simply means: *Copy from the A: drive all files to the C: drive.* It does the exact same thing as...

```
COPY A:\*.* C:\
     │  │  │ └─ ROOT DIRECTORY
     │  │  └ SPACE
     │  └─ ROOT DIRECTORY
     └─ SPACE
```

This version means: *Copy from the A: drive root directory all files to the C: drive root directory.* Although both get the same results, there's an important difference. Can you see it? The directories are specified in the second version.

Admittedly, the extra typing isn't necessary in this example because A: is the same as A:\, and C: is the same as C:\. The root directories of both disks are default (or logged) directories, so DOS automatically uses them. (Refer to how DOS creates a root directory on every disk in Chapter 10 for more on this.) When you want to make sure files are copied to or from a specific directory, though, you must specify it.

If you don't try any of the other examples, do COPY A:*.* C:\DOS. It puts the DOS disk files into the DOS directory on your hard disk. It's convenient to have the files always available.

Directory to Directory Examples

Now, let's take a little test. Do you understand these?

1. COPY   A:*.*   C:\DOS
2. COPY   C:\DOS*.*   A:\
3. COPY   C:*.*   C:\DOS

It helps to read them aloud. BIG HINT: 1. Copies all the files from the root directory of the A: drive into the DOS directory of the C: drive; 2. copies all the files from the DOS directory of the C: drive into the root directory of the A: drive; and, 3. (READ CAREFULLY) copies all the files from the root directory of the C: drive into the DOS directory *in that same drive.*

It all boils down to (a) treating directories like disk drives, and (b) using pathnames. Just as files can be copied from disk to disk, pathnames let you copy from directory to directory.

Okay. You know how you did. Try them on your computer if you care to. The few extra files that result on your disks and directories won't do any harm.

Good news. This gets even easier after you get some experience. And, it gets easier yet when you learn the *command parameter shortcuts* in the Addendum. But, don't bother looking now. There's no rush. Wait until you finish the book.

Almost Ready

Now your hard disk and you are almost ready. There are still some simple steps that will make your computing easier. They're explained in the next two chapters.

(this page is not blank)

12 BACKUP

The Back Up Habit

No, I'm not asking you to get into the habit of starting over. BACK UP means to make a duplicate. When the two words are combined — BACKUP — it *is* a duplicate. Sometimes, the hyphenated BACK-UP appears in print. Since this word is listed in the dictionary, I don't consider it genuine computerese, and don't use it at all.

There are those who are convinced that the only really safe way to back up is to print everything — get it on paper. Data on paper, in computerese, is called a HARD COPY. It's the most impractical backup because restoring data from a hard copy to a disk means keying it into the computer all over again.

Then there are those who believe the safest data protection scheme is to routinely back up all data, and keep several complete backups in more than one place.

Why are people who use computers so concerned about backing up? To provide the best possible chance for data to survive should disaster strike a disk — especially your hard disk.

Disaster!? What kind of disaster?

A disaster can be anything from accidentally erasing one file to disk failure, otherwise known as a CRASH...

CRASH... *inside the computer all the electrons get confused or angry and go on strike. DOS gets stuck. The computer stops computing, and you've got trouble.*

That definition may not be *technically* correct, but the result's the same. If a crash occurs, any data not backed up is lost. How likely is a crash? Well, have you ever heard of MTBF?

MTBF

All disks, floppy or hard, will eventually fail. Manufacturers don't want to make a big deal out of this, so they make a little deal out of it. By a little deal, I mean the value on a hard disk specification sheet listed as MTBF.

The letters MTBF stand for Mean Time Between Failure. And, that stands for the average number of hours a particular disk can be expected to run before failing. The typical hard disk MTBF seems to range between 8,000 and 20,000 hours, the "better quality" hard disks ranging between 30,000 - 40,000 hours. What concerns me about MTBF is the type of averaging used — *mean.*

Of the three types of averaging (mean, median, and mode), the mean can return the highest number from a sample. This is especially so if such a sample includes a few very high numbers, and the rest relatively low. A mean average will produce a higher percentage than the other two. In some circles, choosing to use this most favorable type of averaging is called manipulating statistics.

All this statistic *reveals* is that some disks will last longer than others. Which disk do you have? I don't know about mine, either. I do know that breakdowns and data errors aren't epidemic. It's just that when something does go wrong, believe me, it's always a disaster. One hard disk crash will make a backup believer out of the most cavalier computerist.

Approach the back up habit as you would auto insurance. Get it, but hope you'll never need it.

Back Up Options

Most modern application programs keep data in RAM during work sessions. If the computer loses power, the data in RAM goes to electron heaven, and it doesn't come back.

The back up habit begins, therefore, with periodic *saving* while using an application program. Saving means to record data from RAM onto a disk, and into a file. A resulting work file will eventually be printed, transmitted, or otherwise used for whatever purpose the particular application program was chosen.

With a hard disk, work files are stored in subdirectories. These files are backed up on floppies. There are, basically, two options for backing up a hard disk onto floppies. Either back up the entire disk, or back up files that change.

If you choose to routinely back up your entire hard disk, the process can be unnecessarily time-consuming. For example, backing up ten megabytes of data can easily take over half an hour. If most of the data on the hard disk is application programs, most of the backup time is unnecessary.

The easiest option is to back up the files that change, the work files. Program files don't change, and they're already backed up by the master disks.

One factor that limits your options is the quantity of data to be backed up. If the files to be backed up can fit onto one floppy disk, I recommend you back up with the COPY command.

On the other hand, if the quantity of data to be backed up, whether it's a work file that exceeds the capacity of the backup disk, or more files than will fit, you have no choice but to learn the BACKUP and RESTORE commands.

BACKUP and RESTORE
The "Half-Commands"

BACKUP and RESTORE are specifically designed for backing up a hard disk onto floppies in the built-in drive of a computer. Using these commands, several floppies can be linked to contain any size files, from humble to humongous. BACKUP and RESTORE can also be switched to selectively handle files by subdirectories, modifications, dates, or names.

Think of BACKUP and RESTORE as half-commands because each only does half the job of backing up and restoring data. BACKUP stores files in a unique way, RESTORE is the only way to get them back. One is no good without the other.

Files copied with the BACKUP command can't be used with normal DOS commands, either, until they've been "restored" with the RESTORE command.

Hard DOS It! by Ron Bauer

VERSIONS OF DOS
Don't mix versions of DOS when using the BACKUP and RESTORE commands. Some versions are not compatible with others.

The CHKDSK Command

Using the CHKDSK (CHecK DiSK) command is a wise precaution to take before running the BACKUP command, especially if you intend to back up an entire hard disk. It's also useful for calculating the number of disks you need as backups.

Run the CHKDSK command on your DOS disk right now by putting it into the A: drive, then typing **CHKDSK**, and pressing the **[ENTER]** key...

```
A>CHKDSK
362496 bytes total disk space  <——— DISK STORAGE OF LOGGED DRIVE
 38912 bytes in 3 hidden files <——— Space used by SYSTEM files
264192 bytes in 37 user files  <——— Space used by files
 59392 bytes available on disk <——— Remaining space on disk

655360 bytes total memory <——————— Total RAM
570176 bytes free <——————————————— Available RAM

A> _
```

Check the hard disk from the A: drive by typing **CHKDSK C:**, and pressing the **[ENTER]** key. Or, log onto the hard disk, make DOS the current directory, then enter the CHKDSK command without a parameter. (Aren't you proud? You followed that technical talk without batting an eye.)

NOTE: CHKDSK also reports bad sectors. Some bad sectors are tolerable, and don't necessarily mean the hard disk is damaged.

98

CHKDSK can do more than check and report available disk and RAM space. It can be switched to fix flawed files, too. Just add /F, and run it again. For example, enter **CHKDSK C: /F**. If any problems are found, you'll see a message such as...

```
xxx lost clusters found in xxx chains
Convert lost chains to files (Y/N)?
```

The xxx represents any numbers of "lost clusters" of data. If you answer Y, DOS takes care of needed repairs. It will also list the results.

Repaired files appear in the root directory with names such as FILExxxx.CHK — numbered from 0000 to 9999, hopefully not covering the entire range. The repaired files won't be perfect, but the recovered data can save you time redoing the work. If you're curious, refer to your DOS manual.

If nothing's wrong with the disk, CHKDSK seemingly ignores the /F switch. The apparent lack of response simply means that everything is as fine as CHKDSK can determine.

Here's how to use the CHKDSK report to calculate the number of backup disks needed to back up the entire hard disk.. The formula is simple. Divide the amount of disk space used for files by the number of bytes per backup disk.

For example, suppose CHKDSK shows that 9,109,504 bytes are in user files, and you're using standard 360k floppy disks for backups. Divide 9,109,504 by 360,000 yielding 25.30. You need twenty-six formatted floppy disks to back up these files.

BACKUP Basics

The purpose of BACKUP is to copy data from the hard disk onto one or more floppies. These disks must be formatted. They must also be numbered consecutively, 01, 02, 03, etc., to match the BACKUP prompts. Floppies have less storage space than a hard disk, so as data "spills over" from one disk to the next, BACKUP will prompt you to change disks.

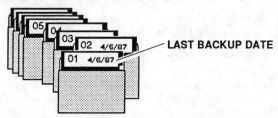

LAST BACKUP DATE

DO-IT-YOURSELF EVER-READY BACKUP KIT

How many should you number? That depends on two things: one, the
quantity of data to be backed up; two, the capacity per floppy. Remember,
you can use CHKDSK to calculate the number needed.

Try a few practice backups. The examples take only minutes because, if
you've been following this book, there's only one file in the root and one
subdirectory on the hard disk.

Mark 01 and 02 on the labels of the formatted disks you prepared in Chapter
Eight. This transforms them into "Practice Backup Disks." With your DOS
disk in the A: drive, you're ready to begin.

Make sure the current directory in the C: drive is the root by typing **CD **,
and pressing the **[ENTER]** key...

```
C>CD \
C> _
```

Log onto the A: drive, then type **BACKUP C: A:**, and press the **[ENTER]**
key...

```
A>BACKUP C: A:

Source disk is Non-Removable

Insert backup diskette 01 in drive A:

Warning!  Files in the target drive
A:\ root directory will be erased
Strike any key when ready
```

THAT MEANS THE
HARD DISK!

Replace the DOS disk in the A: drive with disk 01. Strike a key, and
BACKUP continues...

```
*** Backing up files to drive A: ***
Diskette Number: 01

1-16-86    5:03p    12288    C:\IO.SYS
5-30-85   10:11a    27872    C:\MSDOS.SYS
5-15-85   12:00a    22677    C:\COMMAND.COM

A>_
```

If the files were to overflow the first backup disk, BACKUP would give
you the following message...

```
Insert backup diskette 02 in drive A:

Warning!  Files in the target drive
A:\ root directory will be erased
Strike any key when ready
```

As successive disks fill, BACKUP prompts you to continue replacing one with another, following the numbering scheme, until the hard disk is backed up.

Once BACKUP is finished, run the DIR command on the disk in the A: drive. It shows that only the COMMAND.COM file was backed up...

```
A>DIR

    Volume in drive A has no label
    Directory of A:\

    BACKUPID     @@@      128     4-06-87     2:39a
    COMMAND      COM    22805     5-15-85    12:00a

      2 File(s)            21276767 bytes free
```

It also reveals a special file generated by BACKUP called BACKUPID.@@@. It's a small file that DOS stores on a backup disk to identify the files on it. Also, DOS adds a 128 byte header at the beginning of each backed up file. The header contains the file's path and filename.

The BACKUP command in DOS 3.3 uses a different approach than earlier versions. There are only two files per backup disk regardless of the number of files backed up. One's called BACKUP, the other CONTROL. They contain the backed up files and the backup disk information respectively.

Here's a directory of a DOS 3.3 backup disk ...

```
A>DIR

    Volume in drive A is BACKUP 001
    Directory of A:\

    BACKUP      001     25332     4-6-87     2:39a
    CONTROL     001       243     4-6-87     2:39a
      2 File(s)                 0 bytes free
```

Note that the volume label shows the number of the backup disk. So do both extensions! I suppose saying it three times is to make up for never saying it at all in earlier versions.

Regardless of the DOS version you use, the BACKUP command, without parameters, backs up only the files in the current directory. This means that, by using various parameters, you can selectively back up any data on the hard disk. For example, to back up only the files in one subdirectory, you can choose between two approaches.

One is to make the subdirectory to be backed up the current directory, then enter the standard BACKUP command. For example, to back up all the files in the DOS subdirectory, log onto the C: drive, then make \DOS the current directory...

```
A>C:

C>CD \DOS

C>_
```

Replace the 01 disk in the A: drive with the DOS disk, and log to that drive. Then enter **BACKUP C: A:**...

```
C>A:

A>BACKUP C: A:

Source disk is Non-Removable

Insert backup diskette 01 in drive A:

Warning!  Files in the target drive
A:\ root directory will be erased
Strike any key when ready
```

BACKUP prompts you to put the 01 disk into the A: drive. Do it, then press the **[ENTER]** key. As BACKUP runs, it displays the files being backed up on the screen. You can see that they're the files from the DOS subdirectory. How does BACKUP know to back them up? Because, by default, *BACKUP backs up from the current directory.*

The second way to get the same result takes more typing, but can be accomplished *from any directory.* This time, you tell DOS everything — with specifying parameters.

Begin with the DOS disk in the A: drive. You're still logged onto it, so enter **BACKUP C:\DOS*.* A:**. The results on your screen should be the same as in the first example.

At this point, is the entire hard disk backed up? No, it isn't. When you backed up the DOS subdirectory, you erased the data that was previously backed up from the root directory. Remember the warning? Only the DOS subdirectory is backed up.

Before I show you how to back up the entire hard disk, try one more BACKUP variation. It's a way to back up specific files from one subdirectory, such as the command files from \DOS.

With the DOS disk in the A: drive, enter **BACKUP C:\DOS*.COM A:**.
The command should look like this...

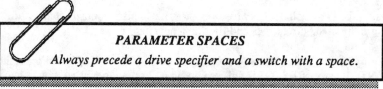

As BACKUP proceeds, you'll see the specific files, those ending in COM, displayed on your screen.

Finally, before going on to the RESTORE procedure, here's the procedure for backing up the entire hard disk, the root directory and all subdirectories.

First, log onto the C: drive, then change the current directory to the root by entering **CD **. You do this because you want to include all files from the root directory, and *BACKUP backs up from the current directory.*

Put the DOS disk into the A: drive, and log to that drive. Type **BACKUP C: A: /S**, and press the **[ENTER]** key. You'll see that this time, everything will be backed up.

> *PARAMETER SPACES*
> *Always precede a drive specifier and a switch with a space.*

RESTORE Basics

Once you've used BACKUP, you need RESTORE to get the backed up data back. The following examples show you how to go about it. If you try them all, you'll probably run RESTORE more times than you'll ever use it in the future. That's because RESTORE is only needed in case of disk or data failure, or if data must otherwise be replaced.

The parameters for RESTORE are almost exactly the opposite of BACKUP. So, other than order, you already know the basics. For example, with the DOS disk in the A: drive, and being logged onto it, entering **RESTORE A: C:**, and pressing the **[ENTER]** key yields the following...

```
A>RESTORE A: C:

Target is Non-Removable            THAT MEANS
                                   THE HARD DISK!

Insert backup diskette 01 in drive A:
Strike any key when ready
```

Replace the DOS disk in the A: drive with backup disk 01, then strike a key...

```
*** Files were backed up (date) ***

*** Restoring files from drive A: ***
Diskette: 01

1-16-86    5:03p   12288    C:\IO.SYS
5-30-85   10:11a   27872    C:\MSDOS.SYS
5-15-85   12:00a   22677    C:\COMMAND.COM
5-15-85   12:00a   22805    C:\DOS\COMMAND.COM
9-18-85    1:09p    2684    C:\DOS\ANSI.SYS
5-14-85   12:02a    1637    C:\DOS\ASSIGN.COM
```

```
10-23-85   3:44p   17104    C:\DOS\XASSIGN.COM
8-27-85    3:08p    7264    C:\DOS\XTREE.COM
1-01-80    1:30a     640    C:\DOS\SCROLL.TXT
          45 File(s)      6144000 bytes free

A>_
```

RESTORE begins restoring files from backup disk 01 into the *current directory* of the hard disk. It doesn't, however, copy any files into this directory if they don't belong there.

So, if you want the subdirectories restored, you must use the /S switch. Using the /S switch not only restores files, it can also reconstruct an entire hierarchy of subdirectories and files on a new hard disk.

With your DOS disk in the A: drive, type RESTORE A: C: /S, and press the [ENTER] key. RESTORE will prompt you. Follow the instructions, then check your results.

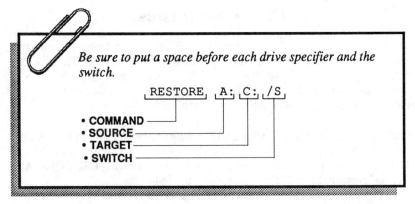

Be sure to put a space before each drive specifier and the switch.

```
RESTORE  A:  C:  /S
```

• COMMAND
• SOURCE
• TARGET
• SWITCH

As RESTORE runs, it reads the instructions in a file header, then restores the file to that subdirectory, displaying the results on the screen. If the sub-directory doesn't exist, it makes a new one. Otherwise, it searches through the backups, prompting you to change backup disks, until the parameter requirements are fulfilled.

If you put a wrong disk into the A: drive, or if it can't find requested files, this message appears...

```
Source does not contain backup files
```

You can selectively restore data by using various parameters — regardless of how you backed up. For example, to restore certain files in one subdirec-tory, you can use wild cards. Here's how to restore all files with an EXE extension in the DOS subdirectory. Put the DOS disk into the A: drive. From the A: drive, enter **RESTORE A: C:\DOS*.EXE**, and press the **[ENTER]** key.

Follow the instructions on your screen.

> *Since this is only practice, checking your results with the DIR command doesn't reflect success or failure because files may or may not be overwritten. If you really want to see RESTORE work, first delete the files from the DOS subdirectory, remove the DOS subdirectory, and delete the COMMAND.COM from the root. Use the DIR com-mand to be sure that all the files are gone. Then RESTORE them.*

Half-Command Switches

Okay, you know how to back up and restore a file, a group of files, a subdirectory, and the entire hard disk. But, there are several alternative ways to get even more control over the BACKUP and RESTORE com-mands. I can't show them all to you because this book is supposed to be easy. And, the easiest way to avoid trouble with switches, or any parame-ters, is to learn only those that apply to your work. You may need only one — or none.

The BACKUP switches are: /S, /A, /M, and /D:<date> Some can be combinations of others.

You've already used the /S switch to back up and restore subdirectories. The only thing to remember about backing up with /S is that, by default, it begins at the current directory. Of course, you can always override a default with a paramater.

?
What's the difference between these?
BACKUP C: A: /S *and* BACKUP C:\ A: /S
In the first version, the backup begins at the current directory of the hard disk. In the second version, the root is specified.

The /A switch means BACKUP will Append, or, in plain words, Add files to the backup disks. No warning appears because using this switch doesn't erase files on the backup disk, it adds them.

BACKUP C:\ A: /S/A

The /M switch means BACKUP backs up only files that have been modified (new or revised) since the last backup. This will only work after it has been used at least once so BACKUP can tell the difference. In other words, the first time you use it, apparently nothing happens. It backs up normally.

BACKUP C:\ A: /S/M

The /D:<date> option backs up only those files that have been changed on or after a specified date. Any files dated on or after the date specified in the parameter will be backed up. The syntax (order of characters) is...

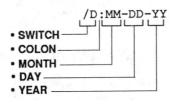

/D:MM-DD-YY
- SWITCH
- COLON
- MONTH
- DAY
- YEAR

Here's an example of specifying filtered files by subdirectory and date range...

BACKUP C:\BOOK\CHAPTERS*.DOC A: /D:4-6-87

Look formidable? C'mon. Read it carefully, aloud, one part at a time. You know this stuff is designed to scare you. So don't be intimidated.

> ### PROBLEMS WITH PARAMETERS?
>
> *Read them aloud — in prose form. This one*
> ***BACKUP C:\BOOK\CHAPTERS*.DOC A:/D:4-6-87***
> *reads "BACKUP from the C: drive in the BOOK subdirectory, in the CHAPTERS subdirectory, all files ending in DOC to the A: drive. Restrict to files dated on or after April 6, 1987."*

The date and time, as well as the /S and /M, switches only work, of course, if you dutifully set the system date each time you boot your computer.

The RESTORE switches are: /S and /P.

The /S switch means RESTORE will restore subdirectories. It begins restoring at the current directory of the hard disk. If a subdirectory doesn't exist, RESTORE makes a new one.

The /P switch means RESTORE will Pause and ask whether a specific file changed since the last backup should be restored. A yes or no answer is all that's required.

The details on the /A, and any of the switches, are in your DOS manual. DOS 3.2 and 3.3 have additional date and time related BACKUP switches. DOS 3.3 also has a "after a date" switch, /A: (date).

> ### DEVELOPING A BACK UP HABIT
>
> *If you're developing a back up routine for a new hard disk, you have the advantage of having to organize only a few files and subdirectories. No harm will be done practicing various BACKUP options to find which suits your needs. The data on your hard disk won't be affected in any way.*

As I said at the outset, there's no sense in trying to learn all the switches now. It will take a while for you to accumulate so many files on your hard disk that you have a need for streamlining the backup process, anyway. If you try to learn them all now, you'll only forget them.

Blow Away Or Archive?

As months of using your computer elapse, superfluous files will accumulate on your hard disk. These should be dealt with or they'll needlessly consume back up time and backup disks. Deal with them in one of two ways. Either blow them away, or archive them.

The meaning of *blow away* should be obvious. But, I'll define it anyway. It means delete or erase those files — send them to electron heaven.

Archiving means to copy important, but no longer active, files onto floppies for storage. Archives should be clearly labelled. So should all removeable media (computerese term that includes floppy disks).

Taking the time to carefully label disks, and date them, is another recommended habit to acquire. Use bold print on labels whenever you have enough room. Colored ink, colored labels, or both, also help you keep track of disks. *Sentinel Technologies* markets high quality disks with brightly colored jackets. Check them out.

Why do I make such a big deal about labels and colors? Because these extra touches help you keep track of data as your disks accumulate. You may only have a few disks now, and can't imagine accumulating an excessive number. You will.

BATCH FILES

A Batch of What?

Occasionally, somebody coining computer terminology, decides to get "user friendly." One such friendly term tossed among the BYTES, BREAKS, and BUFFERS, is BATCH.

Before I came across computers, batch brought only one image into my mind — cookies. Now batch brings two images to mind. The first is still cookies, but sometimes I also think about the special type of file identified by its BAT extension — the batch file.

A batch file is a text file containing *a batch*. A batch is a series of commands and instructions. You can enter the name of a batch file the same way you enter a DOS command, and it will sequentially run its series of commands and instructions in the order in which they are listed in the file.

If you really want to use your hard disk the easy way, let batch files do most of the work for you.

Two Easy BATCH Files

The following examples will give you a "feel" for how batch files function, and what they can do for you. The first batch file example will cause your computer to run some standard DOS commands interactively with you. Since batch files are text, you can use the same method to make batch files that you used in Chapter Nine under the heading "COPY From CON."

Begin in the root directory of your hard disk. Type **COPY CON BATCH.BAT** at the C: prompt, then press the [ENTER] key...

```
C>COPY CON BATCH.BAT
_
```

Then type the following instructions. Put each on its own line by pressing
the [ENTER] key after each: **DATE, TIME, CD \DOS, DIR /P**, and **CD **.
Then press the **F6** key followed by the [ENTER] key. The result should
look like this..

```
DATE
TIME
CD \DOS
DIR /P
CD \
^Z
```

```
1 File(s) copied
```

If you must remake a text file because of a mistake, repeat the COPY file to
CON procedure, making a new version while overwriting the first attempt.
Alternatively, make text files with a text editor, better known as a word
processor, in a non-document or no format mode. Then changes are
simpler.

Whatever method you use, once you have this BATCH.BAT file in the root
directory of your hard disk, type **BATCH** (the extension isn't necessary),
and press the [ENTER] key.

First the date prompt comes up. Don't change it, though you could, just
press the [ENTER] key. Do the same for the time prompt which automatically comes up next. Immediately, a screenful of DOS commands scrolls
up and pauses. Go through the entire directory by following the screen
prompts. At the end of the directory, DOS makes the root the current
directory.

Practice running BATCH.BAT several times. Try to picture each command
as DOS runs it. Once you feel comfortable with BATCH.BAT, try the next
example.

An Easy Way to Back Up

Imagine entering one or two characters instead of a string of commands,
parameters, and switches every time you back up. Here's an example of a
file that can do just that. Granted, it only copies a few files from the DOS
subdirectory, but the idea is what matters.

This batch file is called BU.BAT. The BU stands for back up. To make
this file, type **COPY CON BU.BAT**, and press the [ENTER] key...

```
C>COPY CON BU.BAT

-
```

Then type **CD \DOS, BACKUP C:\DOS*.COM A:, CD **, pressing the
[ENTER] key at the end of each line. Then press the **F6** key followed by
the [ENTER] key. Your results should look like this..

```
CD \DOS
BACKUP C:\DOS\*.COM A:
CD \
^Z
```

Put one of your backup disks from Chapter Twelve into the A: drive, then
type **BU**, and press the [ENTER] key. You know what to do from here,
don't you? You sit back and watch DOS do your work for you.

True, it takes some time to prepare such a batch file. But it's worth the
preparation time because it will make your back up habit easier to acquire.

The AUTOEXEC.BAT File

Here's a batch file that you can make right away, and benefit from every
day. Its purpose is to automatically take care of routine start-up procedures.
It's called AUTOEXEC.BAT...

> ***AUTOEXEC.BAT****... a file that "AUTOmatically EXECutes a
> BATch of commands" when you boot a computer.*

Before you make an AUTOEXEC.BAT file for your hard disk, however,
you should know about the PATH and PROMPT commands.

The PATH Command

You already know that, by default, DOS searches for commands in the
current directory of the logged drive. You also know that you must change
to a directory in order to use a command in it.

If DOS can't find a command, either it's not in the current directory of the
logged drive, it was typed incorrectly, or there's no such command. DOS
responds to any of these eventualities with the following message...

```
Bad command or file name.
```

You know all this. Right? Well, now I must tell you that there's a way to
instruct DOS to search for commands in specific directories *other* than the
current directory. You can do it with the PATH command.

The PATH command defines a search path for DOS. Enter any directories after the PATH command, and they become part of the "path of DOS's search." Then, any time an executable file (one ending in EXE, COM, or BAT) is entered, DOS will look for it in those directories. What will DOS do if it finds that executable file? Yes. It will execute it!

For example, the CHKDSK command won't run unless the CHKDSK.COM file is in the current directory of the logged drive. Test this to be sure.

Now, watch what happens if the DOS subdirectory which contains this file, is in the search path. First, put it in the search path by typing **PATH C:\DOS**, and pressing the **[ENTER]** key...

```
C>PATH C:\DOS

C> _
```

Although it doesn't look like anything's happened, it has. DOS will now search for executable files in the current directory *and* the DOS subdirectory. Try it. First, make sure you're in the root directory, then type **CHKDSK**, and press the **[ENTER]** key.

Preparing and appending the search path is easy. Type PATH followed by a space, then the subdirectory pathname. Don't use spaces, but do separate each pathname with a semicolon.

Traditionally, the first pathname should be the hard disk root directory, C:\. Next comes the DOS subdirectory pathname. Enter them now by typing **PATH C:\;C:\DOS**, then pressing the **[ENTER]** key...

```
C>PATH C:\;C:\DOS

C> _
```

Again, it doesn't look like anything's happened. To check the active search path, at the prompt, type **PATH**, and press the **[ENTER]** key...

```
C>PATH
PATH=C:\;C:\DOS
```

Do you clearly understand the various meanings of the term PATH?

PATH... *search path command.*

PATH MARKER... *back slash preceded by one or more characters.*

PATHNAME... *complete file or directory name including the names of any directories leading to it.*

The PROMPT Command

The default DOS prompt is made up of two characters, the "name of the logged drive" and "greater than" sign. When A: is the logged drive, you see A>. When C: is the logged drive, you see C>.

Using the PROMPT command, you can perk up your prompt. You can make it say things other than A> and C>. It can be informative, cute, nagging, or sincere. For example, it could greet you with *How may I serve you, master?* or *Don't forget to enter your LOG!* or *Is it time to take a break, yet?* or just about anything. But, I'm getting ahead of myself.

The PROMPT command parameters are *strings* (computerese for any number of characters following one another) of text which sometimes include code characters, called (but not by me) *metastrings*. Each code character must be preceded by (what else?!) a *metacharacter*. The code character prefix is a dollar ($) sign.

The doing is easier than the explaining, so try a few examples. First, make sure you're logged to the DOS subdirectory by typing **CD \DOS**, and pressing the **[ENTER]** key. Then type **PROMPT $P**, and press the **[ENTER]** key again...

```
C>CD \DOS

C>PROMPT $P
C:\DOS _
```

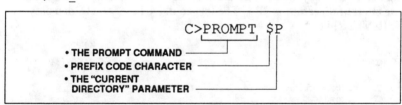

```
                    C>PROMPT $P

  • THE PROMPT COMMAND
  • PREFIX CODE CHARACTER
  • THE "CURRENT
    DIRECTORY" PARAMETER
```

Press the **[ENTER]** key two or three times. You'll see that C:\DOS continues to be your new prompt.

Now try something else. Type **PROMPT NG**, and press the **[ENTER]** key...

```
C:\DOS PROMPT $N$G
C> _
```

```
                    C>PROMPT $N$G

  • THE PROMPT COMMAND
  • THE "LOGGED DRIVE"
    PARAMETER
  • THE "GREATER THAN" PARAMETER
```

Back where you started, right? If you're not sure how this works yet, stay with me. It'll all fall into place soon. This time, try setting the prompt to remind you of both the current directory and the logged drive. Type **PROMPT P_NG**, and press the **[ENTER]** key...

```
C>PROMPT $P$_$N$G
C:\DOS
C> _
```

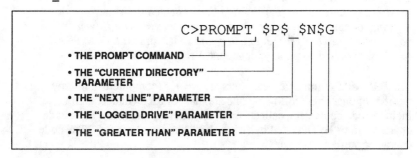

```
        C>PROMPT $P$_$N$G

 • THE PROMPT COMMAND
 • THE "CURRENT DIRECTORY"
   PARAMETER
 • THE "NEXT LINE" PARAMETER
 • THE "LOGGED DRIVE" PARAMETER
 • THE "GREATER THAN" PARAMETER
```

Clear the screen (CLS) to see how this prompt looks by itself. Then change back to the root directory by typing **CD **, and pressing the **[ENTER]** key...

```
C:\DOS
C>CD \
C:\
C>_
```

Got the idea? Okay, now comes the nifty part. This time type **PROMPT The current directory is $P $_The logged drive is...$_NG**, and press the **[ENTER]** key...

```
C:\
C>PROMPT The current directory is $P $_The logged drive is...$_$N$G

The current directory is C:\
The logged drive is...
C> _
```

I recommend you use this prompt all the while you're learning to use hard disk directories, even after. With it, regardless of how many subdirectories are in your hard disk, you can't get disoriented. As a bonus, the repetition of seeing this information helps you become familiar with important jargon (an oxymoron?).

You can use it even if you're working with someone else's computer. It takes but a moment to key it in at the DOS prompt. You can return to the traditional prompt by booting the computer, or by entering the PROMPT command without parameters.

As I said at the beginning of this discussion of this section, you can customize your prompt in hundreds of ways. The various parameters are in your DOS operator manual. Here's a partial list for handy reference...

The PROMPT Command Reference
1. *$ prefix code character (metacharacter)*
2. *N (Name of) the logged drive*
3. *P the current (Path) directory*
4. *_ to begin a new line*
5. *G the "Greater than" (>) sign*
6. *D the Date*
7. *T the Time*
8. *V the Version of DOS*

There are other commands, such as ECHO and REM, for putting custom text into various DOS operations. For information on how to do it, refer to your DOS manual.

That's all there is to it. However, as with the PATH command, the PROMPT modifications must be entered each time you boot unless you store them in an AUTOEXEC.BAT file.

How to Make An AUTOEXEC.BAT

You make the AUTOEXEC.BAT file the same way you made the previous batch files. Yep. That's all there is to it, except for what goes inside. This one will contain a PATH and a PROMPT to fit the hard disk setup you've developed so far.

Put each command on a line of its own. Enter the PATH command with search path parameters on line 1. Enter the PROMPT command with a customized prompt on line 2. Enter the clear screen command (optional) on line 3. And, enter **F6**, the end of file instruction, on line 4. Use the following illustration as reference...

```
C>COPY CON AUTOEXEC.BAT
PATH C:\;C:\DOS
PROMPT The current directory is $P $_The logged drive is...$_$N$G
CLS
^Z
C>_
```

That's it.

Time To Boot

You can run the AUTOEXEC.BAT file like any other batch file by entering AUTOEXEC. The extension isn't necessary. The AUTOEXEC.BAT is different in that it executes automatically whenever you boot. Do either a WARM or a COLD boot, now. Leave the door of the A: drive open, though, so DOS will boot from the hard disk.

When an AUTOEXEC.BAT or any other batch file runs, DOS echoes the results on your screen, so you can visually confirm the process. If a command fails to function, DOS reports the error in the same way as when it's manually entered.

Check your typing. Remember, you can look at your results at any time by entering **COPY AUTOEXEC.BAT CON**, or by using a word processor.

Ways to Stop a BATCH File

When you enter the DIR command, DOS runs it, and the list of files scrolls up the screen. You can stop and start a scrolling screen with [CTRL] S (Refer to Chapter Seven). Sometimes, though, you won't want to continue a scroll at all. You want to forget it. Use [CTRL] C to CANCEL the process.

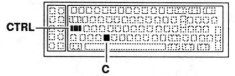

CTRL

C

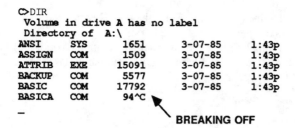

NOTE: Your keyboard layout may not match the illustration. Due to new keyboard designs, the locations of special keys vary.

Log onto the DOS directory. Type **DIR**, and press the [ENTER] key...

```
C>DIR
 Volume in drive A has no label
 Directory of  A:\
ANSI     SYS      1651      3-07-85      1:43p
ASSIGN   COM      1509      3-07-85      1:43p
ATTRIB   EXE     15091      3-07-85      1:43p
BACKUP   COM      5577      3-07-85      1:43p
BASIC    COM     17792      3-07-85      1:43p
BASICA   COM        94^C
_
```

BREAKING OFF

Once the scrolling begins, quickly press [CTRL] C. When the cancel occurs, a ^C appears. The ^ represents the [CTRL] key, the C represents the C.

[CTRL] [BREAK] does the same thing. It means "BREAK OFF" or "Put on the BRAKES." (I invented the last two definitions.)

I think of [CTRL] C as a "panic" command because it's the only way to interrupt the relentless running of a batch command. When you use it this way, you see the prompt...

```
Terminate batch job (Y/N)?
```

Press **Y**, and the [ENTER] key. It's that easy.

GENERAL RULES FOR A BATCH FILE

1. It must be an ASCII (no format/non-document) text file.
2. Each command must be on a separate line.
3. It must end with a BAT extension.

Automatic System Configuration

An important file that seems similar to AUTOEXEC.BAT is CONFIG.SYS. CONFIG.SYS modifies the way a computer's memory works, loads programs that control some hardware devices, and does some other technical things that won't be described in this book.

Although it doesn't have a BAT extension, CONFIG.SYS is similar to AUTOEXEC.BAT in several ways. It must be in the root directory, it automatically customizes the computer during the booting process, and it can be edited as a text file. The only significant difference is that most of the commands it contains can't be executed any other way. They must be in the CONFIG.SYS file for DOS to use them.

The default BUFFERS and FILES settings in most computers aren't adequate for some high-powered applications. Changes for these settings go in a CONFIG.SYS file.

The BUFFERS setting tells DOS to set aside more blocks of memory for DOS to access instead of the disk. Without going into detail, this increases disk performance with some applications. If I'm starting to get a little technical here, forgive me. I was curious about this one, so I looked it up in my DOS manual.

The FILES setting tells DOS how many files it can open at one time. Some applications use twenty or more files simultaneously. Most systems have fewer than ten as the default.

How many FILES and BUFFERS go in the CONFIG.SYS file? The settings are supplied by the application programs that need them. Sometimes the application programs automatically make or modify a CONFIG.SYS file during installation. Other times, they include instructions for you to do the work.

You make a CONFIG.SYS file the same way you make batch files. The contents of such a file might look like this...

```
FILES=20
BUFFERS=15
```

You also need a CONFIG.SYS file when you add a device (Refer to Chapter Nine) to your system. One popular device is a MOUSE...

MOUSE... *a mechanical adjunct to the keyboard which moves a screen pointer in response to physical movements across a flat surface.*

Being a device, a mouse must be defined as such in the CONFIG.SYS file. Typically, it looks like this...

```
FILES=20
BUFFERS=15
DEVICE=MOUSE
```

When the CONFIG.SYS file contains a DEVICE requirement, it looks on the disk for a DEVICE DRIVER...

DEVICE DRIVER... *a short program that tells DOS how to handle input and output of a device.*

The combination of CONFIG.SYS and the device driver software links the device to DOS. The device then becomes part of the system.

That's all you *need* to know about CONFIG.SYS. That's all I know about it, and I use, and have used, most of the popular application programs on the market. Any special instructions for using CONFIG.SYS or any other files that come with an application program are part of the installation procedure. Read the manual!

NOTE: Whenever you add or modify a CONFIG.SYS file, reboot your computer to instruct DOS that operational changes have been made.

Special System Configuration

Although PC- and MS-DOS computers are standardized to be IBM-compatible, sometimes certain hardware components need special attention. Two such components are the internal battery-operated clock and the hard disk parking system.

Most modern computers automatically manage both loading the internal battery-operated clock and parking the hard disk. The operator manual that accompanies a computer explains any such hardware variations, but you won't notice them if you don't know to look.

For example, some internal battery-operated clocks need start and set programs on the boot disk. These programs might also require triggering commands in either the AUTOEXEC.BAT or the CONFIG.SYS files.

Sometimes, the presence of the AUTOEXEC.BAT file is enough for DOS to automatically enter the DATE and TIME commands. Without this batch file, DOS will present you with the date and time prompts as part of the booting procedure.

NO INTERNAL CLOCK?

If you don't have an internal battery-operated clock, put the DATE and TIME commands in your AUTOEXEC.BAT file. Without an internal clock or these commands, DOS does not set nor prompt you to set the system clock on some computers.

The PARK Command

Parking the hard disk means to move the read/write heads to a safety zone — an area without data — and "parking" them there. Parking is an essential safety precaution to avoid permanent damage to the data or disk if the hardware is bumped or moved.

You mechanically park the heads of a hard disk — one that needs to be parked — with a command called PARK. Just enter PARK and follow the screen instructions, which are usually "Turn Off Power Now." When power is restored to the hard disk, the heads return to normal operation.

The PARK command sometimes has other names such as PARKDISK, SHIPDISK, or something similar. Whatever the parking procedure that accompanies your system, make sure you know what it is, and how to use it.

In The Near Future...

Using batch files makes computing so easy, you'll almost find it embarrassing to accept all the compliments you'll collect from fawning admirers. One way to learn more about batch files is to peek into those that come with various applications, such as the installation files. Use the DIR command to find the names of any files ending with BAT.

APPLICATION PROGRAMS

You should include the subdirectory pathnames of any application programs you intend to store in your hard disk. Check the operating manual of your application programs to be sure they're compatible with the DOS search path feature.

I hate to say it, but batch files can be fun! Understanding batch files can give you a good sense of the relative value of software and hardware, too. Think about it. What can a computer *really* do without precise instructions?

REVIEW & REFERENCE

The Essential Eleven
&
The Additional Eight

If you're someone who's been struggling with DOS for a while, picked up this book and flipped to this chapter for some quick answers, *perhaps* that's okay. *Perhaps* this is the only chapter you need because it's an overview.

But, if you want to learn to use DOS the easy way, and stop that struggling, I recommend you first read *Easy DOS It!*, then — if you use a hard disk — read this book from the beginning.

DOS commands are either INTERNAL or EXTERNAL.

INTERNAL commands automatically load when you boot the computer. They don't appear in directories because they reside in the RAM of the computer. These commands are always available at any system prompt. Internal is sometimes called MEMORY RESIDENT.

An EXTERNAL command is outside the RAM of the computer. The file must be available on a disk in the logged drive.

With a hard disk, the command must be either in the current directory, or available through the PATH command.

The Essential Eleven

1. DATE
(See *Easy DOS It!* Chapter Six)

An internal command. At the system prompt, you can use this command to check or change the current date.

2. TIME
(See Easy DOS It! Chapter Six)

An internal command. At the system prompt, you can use this command to check or change the current time.

3. DIR
(See Easy DOS It! Chapters Seven and Nine)

An internal command. At the system prompt, you can use this command to see a list of the files of a disk in any drive.

(Use WILD CARDS to filter for specific files.)

(DIR/P will PAUSE a scrolling directory. DIR/W will show filenames and extensions only.)

4. CHKDSK
(See Easy DOS It! Addendum)
(See Hard DOS It! Chapter Twelve)

An external command. At the system prompt, you can use this utility program to check a specified disk for the amount of used and available space. It also shows the amount of used and available RAM.

5. FORMAT
(See Easy DOS It! Chapter Eight)
(See Hard DOS It! Chapter Eight)

An external command. At the system prompt, you can use this utility program to have DOS analyze a new or used disk for defective tracks, initialize a directory, set up file allocations, and make other technical modifications in preparation for storing files.

FORMAT prepares disks for storing files.

(FORMAT/S adds COMMAND.COM and hidden system files.) With a hard disk, with DOS in the PATH, you can copy the system files to any directory or disk in another drive.

> NOTE: *Some computer systems use the term INITIALIZE which is basically the same function as formatting.*

6. DISKCOPY
*(See **Easy DOS It!** Chapter Eight)*
*(See **Hard DOS It!** Chapter Eight)*

An external command. At the system prompt, you can use this command to make a duplicate of any disk. DISKCOPY also formats blank disks before copying.

> *NOTE: FORMAT and DISKCOPY erase all data from a disk.*

7. DISKCOMP
*(See **Easy DOS It!** Chapter Eight)*
*(See **Hard DOS It!** Chapter Eight)*

An external command. At the system prompt, you can use this command to compare two disks sector by sector.

DISKCOMP will only recognize exact duplicates as "ok."

8. COPY
*(See **Easy DOS It!** Chapter Nine)*
*(See **Hard DOS It!** Chapter Nine)*

An internal command. At the system prompt, you can use this command to copy one or more files to or from disks and devices. While copying, you can also change filenames and combine files.

(Use the WILD CARD characters, the * and the ? to save typing and time.)

9. ERASE or DEL
*(See **Easy DOS It!** Chapter Nine)*
*(See **Hard DOS It!** Chapter Nine)*

An internal command. At the system prompt, you can use this command to erase one or more files. NOTE: You can substitute DEL (DELete) for ERASE. DOS recognizes either.

(Use WILD CARDS to ERASE several files at once.)

10. RENAME or REN
*(See **Easy DOS It!** Chapter Nine)*
*(See **Hard DOS It!** Chapter Nine)*

An internal command. At the system prompt, you can use this command to change a file's name.

> *NOTE: Save yourself three keystrokes by using REN instead of RENAME.*

11. SYS
*(See **Easy DOS It!** Chapter Nine and the Addendum)*
*(See **Hard DOS It!** Chapter Nine)*

An external command. At the system prompt, you can copy the DOS system files from the DOS disk.

The Additional Eight

1. \ (backslash)
(See Chapter Eleven)

The \ isn't officially a command, but for all its importance, perhaps it should be considered one. If this symbol is omitted, or used incorrectly, some commands simply won't work.

If this were truly a command, it would be internal. Alone it means Root Directory. Preceded by a symbol, it means Path marker.

2. MD (Make Directory) (MKDIR)
(See Chapter Eleven)

An internal command. This is the command for making a SUBdirectory.

3. CD (Change Directory) (CHDIR)
(See Chapter Eleven)

An internal command. This is the command for changing from one directory to another. Entered without a parameter, it displays the current directory.

4. RD (Remove Directory) (RMDIR)
(See Chapter Eleven)

An internal command. This is the command for removing a SUBdirectory.

5. BACKUP / RESTORE
"half-commands"
(See Chapter Twelve)

These are external commands. The BACKUP command copies files and directories from a hard disk onto floppies, tape, or other storage media. The RESTORE command is necessary for retrieving the backed up data. It's only necessary if data must be restored or moved to another disk. With luck, you'll never use this command.

6. PATH
(See Chapter Thirteen)

An internal command. This command tells DOS in which directories to search for executable files, eliminating the need for frequent directory changing.

7. PROMPT
(See Chapter Thirteen)

An internal command. This command changes the system prompt display.

8. PARK
(See Chapter Thirteen)

This is an external command. Its purpose is to instruct a mechanism in the hard disk to move the heads to a "safe" area on the disk so no physical damage can occur to it when it's powered down. When power is restored to the hard disk, the heads return to normal operation. Some computers use a non-DOS version of this command. Newer hard disks don't require this command at all. The heads automatically park and lock when power is lost, or when the hard disk hasn't been accessed for a five or ten second interval.

That's them... The "Essential Eleven" and The "Additional Eight."

For some relevant details and tips, turn to the Addendum.

(ditto re page 94)

ADDENDUM

Here are a few, important supplemental ideas and tips you may need from time to time. You won't need them often, but when you do, they're indispensable.

Specifying Drives and Subdirectories

No sooner do I proclaim this addendum to contain items you won't use often, I present one that you probably will. It's a typing shortcut for use with the COPY, DIR, and ERASE commands.

As you know, DOS uses the default drive or current directory if you don't specify something else. So, save yourself some typing by not specifying the logged drive or the current directory because DOS uses it anyway. Here are some examples...

Standard	Simplified
A>COPY A:SCROLL.TXT C:	A>COPY SCROLL.TXT C:
A>COPY A:*.* C:	A>COPY *.* C:
A>COPY C:SCROLL.TXT A:	A>COPY C:SCROLL.TXT
A>DEL A:*.TXT	A>DEL *.TXT
A>DIR A:	A>DIR

In case you don't see the differences, look at the A: drive specifier in the first line of the Standard column. Look for it in the first line of the Simplified column. Get it? Okay. Repeat with each line. The instructions in both columns are identical.

More DOS Commands?

This book covers fewer than half of the standard DOS commands. Probably, you'll never need to learn the rest of them. However, there are a few that may be of interest to you. They're not essential, so I'll only allude to them. They are: TYPE, TREE, MODE, PRINT, and XCOPY.

The TYPE Command

This command "types" the contents of a file onto the screen.

TYPE SCROLL.TXT

This is similar to COPY SCROLL.TXT CON that was explained in Chapter Nine. The result is identical. This command simply uses fewer keystrokes. Compare COPY SCROLL.TXT CON with TYPE SCROLL.TXT. See? You can save yourself the extra effort of typing three characters, if that sort of thing interests you.

The TREE Command

Use the TREE command to see a list of subdirectories. Just enter TREE at the prompt. If you want to see subdirectories *and* files, add the /F switch. The listing scrolls by fast, so use [CTRL] S to stop it when desired.

If you want to print the listing, enter the command this way...

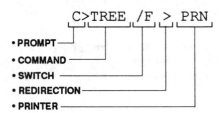

The > (greater than) symbol used this way "redirects" the output from the standard direction to a specified target. The standard direction is to the display. In this example, it's redirected to the default printer. If you want to learn more about redirection, refer to your DOS manual.

MODE vs MODEM

MODE and MODEM seem similar somehow, don't they? There's only a one character difference between them. But, there are clear differences. One is a DOS command, the other's a hardware device.

The MODE command sets communications parameters at a serial PORT...

> **PORT...** *a connector at the rear or side of a computer for the exchange of data with other hardware. The serial ports are COM1: and COM2:.*

The MODE command usually goes in the AUTOEXEC.BAT file. Its parameters are baud rate, parity, data bits, stop bits, and type of device. A device can be a serial printer, a mouse, or a MODEM.

A MODEM is telecommunications hardware that can be internal or external. MODEM stands for MOdulate-DEModulate. Modulate means change data so it can be sent over telephone systems, and demodulate means change data so it can be used by the computer. For more about MODEMS, refer to *The EASY MODEM & FAX Book* by Ron Bauer.

The PRINT Command

Simply put, you can print files with this command. But, it's better to use a word processor or the print function of a software application because PRINT prints a non-formatted version of a file. This command is useful, however, for "quick and dirty" hard copies.

The XCOPY Command

This variation of the COPY command is available with DOS versions 3.2 and higher. Using XCOPY is a good way to back up work because it copies files *and* subdirectories. It's faster than the COPY command, and it uses switches similar to those of the BACKUP command.

I use XCOPY often, especially for backing up subdirectories containing text files.

Check Your DOS Version

When using program disks from other computers, certain DOS commands may give you the message *Wrong DOS version*. This means you're trying to use a DOS command on a disk that's incompatible with the version used to boot the system.

Which version of DOS is in use? At the system prompt, type **VER**, and press the **[ENTER]** key. DOS will tell you.

Diagnostics

Most hardware manufacturers provide DIAGNOSTIC software of some sort. Sometimes it's a disk that came with your master DOS disk. Sometimes it's just a file on the DOS disk called TEST, or something similar.

Use the diagnostic software to check that everything you bought is there, and it all works. Your computer manual provides the information you need to run the diagnosis. Usually, step-by-step instructions are on the screen and are invariably easy to follow.

In all the DIAGNOSTIC and TEST programs I've tried, the only term I found puzzling was "scratch disk." This is merely computerese for "a disk that you don't mind erasing."

PrtSc

[SHIFT] [PrtSc] is the PRinT Screen command. It's on your keyboard, usually to the right.

Press either of the [SHIFT] keys, and the [PrtSc] key. (Some new keyboards have a Print Scrn key that works without the shift key.) The display on your screen will be sent to the default printer port. The computerese for this is "screen dump." Classy, huh?

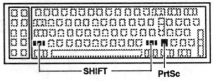

SHIFT — PrtSc

[CTRL] [PrtSc] will send all characters that appear on your screen to your printer as you work. For example, you can print a scrolling directory this way. Press these keys again to turn off this function. Who knows, maybe this will be useful to you sometime?!

MORE HARDWARE

A few additional pieces of hardware can make your computer more versatile and easier to use. I'll mention only a few of them, and only touch on what they can do because details about them are beyond the scope of this book.

Other Removable Media

In general, you have two choices for backup media, floppies or something else. I back up exclusively on floppies because that's the type of drive that came with the computers I use.

One item under the "something else" heading is the *streaming tape backups* medium. *Streaming tape backup* hardware is similar to an extra disk drive exclusively for backup, except that it uses magnetic tape cartridges instead of disks. This is an extra cost option that is useful for backing up very large capacity hard disks.

Floppy disks and tape cartridges are removable media for storing data. There are others, too, such as the Bernoulli Box replaceable cartridge and even videotape. If you're interested in these devices, check with a hardware dealer.

More RAM

The subject of RAM is changing fast. When MS-DOS computers were first on the market, 64k of RAM was enough to run most programs. But times have changed, and they're still a changin'. Even being equipped with the maximum amount of RAM for MS- and PC-DOS computers, 640 kilobytes, may not be enough to make your system perform like the ads on TV. Now the newest hardware and software needs more. Megabytes has replaced kilobytes as the unit of memory measurement. Today's application programs are only friendly in exchange for large amounts of RAM and disk space.

Check carefully how much RAM is needed for ALL the programs you intend to use. You may need to add hardware to your computer called "memory boards." These provide extra RAM so you can have such power features as EXTENDED and EXPANDED memory.

The extra memory is usually needed if you want to take advantage of CACHE and RAMDISK techniques for speeding up the operation of your computer. The speedier operation relates to faster access to the drives, not to how fast the computer will calculate or otherwise respond to commands.

Finally...

The temptation is great to describe more and more of the options available for personal computers. But, I'm stopping here.

If you want to learn more about these technologies, you'll have to do some studying on your own, I'm afraid. *Microsoft Press* publishes several good books on DOS and various software and hardware applications, and there are other sources.

My purpose has been to help you quickly gain competence with a computer in the easiest possible way. Limiting the commands, the *Essential Eleven* and *Additional Eight*, has done it for others, so it will likely do it for you. Even if you need to know more, you'll find that this approach makes it easier for you to understand that, too.

(ditto re page 94)

HARD DISK DESCRIPTION

This appendix answers the questions...

1. Do you care about the inner workings of hard disks?

2. Has someone stuck you with the job to INSTALL your hard disk?

What IS a Hard Disk?

Until a few years ago, the only drives available for MS- and PC-DOS computers were those using removable floppy disks. Then IBM made the Winchester available. The term Winchester was the project name for a sealed drive and disk assembly which was a combination of two 30 megabyte disk designs. Combined, they were 30-30. Get it? That's the caliber of the famous Winchester rifle. Movie cowboys still use them to lever bullets onto the ground when they want to look intense.

Just to keep the computerese consistently inconsistent, IBM now calls the Winchester a FIXED DISK. Perhaps because it and its drive remain fixed inside the computer. It also occasionally refers to this type of drive as "non-removable." But, there's yet a more popular name for the Winchester, non-removable, fixed disk, and the one I choose to use throughout this book — HARD DISK.

I doubt you'll ever see the interior of a hard disk because it's sealed in its own drive, and can't be removed. Moreover, most people couldn't care less what's inside anyway, so long as it works. However, you're reading this appendix, so you must be at least mildly curious about how a hard disk can hold so much and be so fast. Okay. You asked for it.

To begin, a hard disk is actually several rigid disks, or platters, stacked one onto another. Platters are rigid rather than flexible, as are floppy disks, and are either plated or coated with a magnetic material.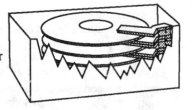

The platters are mounted on a motor-driven spindle which turns twelve times faster than a standard floppy drive hub. Read/write heads, one for each surface of each platter, are attached to an arm assembly.

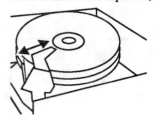

Because they're part of an assembly, the arms move as a unit. The fast spin rate and multiple read/write heads mean more disk surface can be reached in less time than with floppy drives.

Two other reasons a hard disk is so fast are because it's always turning and the heads never touch the surfaces. The floppy disk must start from a standstill then get up to speed before an appointed spot can be located by the read/write heads. The hard disk read/write heads, on their mechanical arms, can rapidly sweep the surfaces of the spinning platters.

Floppy read/write heads are in contact with the disk surface. The read/write heads of hard disk drives, however, travel an almost microscopic distance above the surface of the platters.

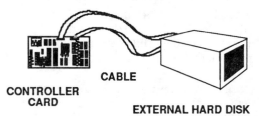

CABLE

CONTROLLER CARD

EXTERNAL HARD DISK

One other element affecting the speed and operation of a hard disk is its controller card.

Many computer systems use external hard disks. An external hard disk is in

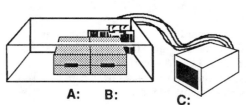

A: B: C:

a cabinet which also contains a cooling fan and a power supply. The unit is cabled to the computer, and connected to a controller card.

Most systems today, however, house the hard disk assembly and controller inside the computer cabinet.

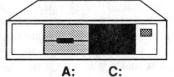

To sum up the general description of a hard disk, it's comprised of four main parts: platters, heads, drive motor, and electronic drive controller. There's also a power supply, but this depends on whether the drive is internal or external.

Finally, there's the "hard card." It's a hard disk that's been miniaturized in physical size only. The capacities are the same as standard hard disks.

DISK **CONTROLLER SECTION**

It comes complete on the card, no cables needed.

A Typical Hard Disk System

I'm sure you know whether or not your computer system includes a hard disk. If not, the usual tip-off is the number of floppy disk drives. If there are two, you probably don't have a hard disk. In that case, you're reading the wrong chapter.

On the other hand, if your system has one floppy drive, it probably also has a hard disk hidden inside. Just for reference, here are two examples...

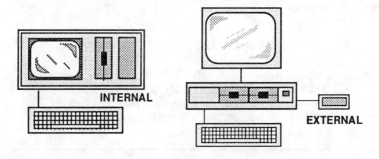

INTERNAL

EXTERNAL

The size of your hard disk doesn't matter as far as the instructions in this book go. At one time, a 10 megabyte hard disk seemed more than enough storage space for a PC. Now, 20 megabytes is common, 40 is moving up fast, and who knows what the new standard will be.

Installing a Hard Disk

A hard disk, before being submitted to the FORMAT command, must be installed mechanically and electronically. The necessary installation should be done before you get it, either at the factory or by your dealer.

The mechanical installation is putting hardware into hardware; the hard disk into the computer. It includes making all necessary connections. It's a technical procedure that I recommend you leave to technically trained people.

Electronic installation is a term peculiar to computer technology. The FORMAT command completely takes care of electronically installing floppy disks, but not a hard disk. A hard disk requires three types of formatting. The first is called the Low Level Format.

Low Level Format

The Low Level Format (sometimes called PHYSICAL format) requires using a DOS program called DEBUG, and instructions specific to the particular hard disk to be installed. The procedure magnetically marks the disk surfaces and allocates the part of the disk for DOS to store essential data used for booting and recording directories. This is also the location of the FAT — File Allocation Tables. If DOS can't find the FAT, you can't find anything on the hard disk!

Most hard disks, particularly the internal type, are now supplied with the Low Level Format done for you. It's just as well. It takes a technician to do it right, anyway.

The FDISK Command

The second type of formatting is called FDISK. The FDISK command is on your DOS disk. FDISK means FIXED DISK, or it means FIX disk. I'll guess the latter because some *fixing* is necessary before using the FORMAT command for the first time. Actually, FDISK might be better named PDISK, the P standing for PARTITION...

PARTITION... *A section of a hard disk used by a single operating system, in our case, MS- or PC-DOS. Each partition acts as an individual disk drive. A hard disk must be partitioned even for only one partition.*

If you have a hard disk larger than thirty megabytes, it must have more than one partition. The second partition is usually called the D: drive.

The majority of computer users never need to learn the FDISK command any more than they need the details on Low Level Formatting. Actually, I think this subject is only useful for chats at computer stores. But, just for reference, I'll briefly describe the process.

NOTE: FROM THIS POINT ON, I'M ASSUMING YOU'RE USING AN INSTALLED, 10 TO 30 MEGABYTE HARD DISK, BLANK OR CONTAINING NO IMPORTANT DATA.

With your DOS disk in the A: drive, and being logged to that drive, type **FDISK**, then press the **[ENTER]** key...

```
A>FDISK

IBM Personal Computer
Fixed Disk Setup Program Version 3.10
(C)Copyright 1983, 1984
FDISK Options
Choose one of the following:

    1.   Create DOS partition
    2.   Change Active Partition
    3.   Delete DOS Partition
    4.   Display Partition Date
    5.   Select Next Fixed Disk

Enter choice: [1]

Press Esc to return to DOS
```

I'm only going to discuss the default option, number one, so press the **[ENTER]** key...

```
Create DOS Partition

Current Fixed Disk Drive: 1
Partition    Status    Type    Start    End    Size
    1          A        DOS       0      304    305

Total disk space is  305 cylinders
The current active partition is 1

Fixed disk already has a DOS partition.

Press ESC to return to FDISK Options
```

Unless you have a good reason to do otherwise, make the entire disk one partition. The default is Yes, so press the **Y** key. DOS displays...

    Are you sure? (Y/N)

Yes. You're sure. Press the **Y** key...

    Formatting...

This looks like the message you get when formatting a floppy disk, doesn't it? That's why I call it the second type of formatting. In a few moments you see...

    System will now restart
    Insert DOS diskette in Drive A:
    Press any key when ready...

The system will boot from the DOS disk in the A: drive when you press any key. When booted, the hard disk is the C: drive by default. DOS named it for you.

Now it's time for the third, and final, phase of preparing a hard disk, probably the only one you'll ever use. Just as the Low Level Format had a technical name, PHYSICAL, the standard formatting has one, too. It's called LOGICAL. Great name, huh? I don't know what it means, either. The procedure, though, is the same as formatting a floppy disk. So, turn back to Chapter Eight, beginning on page 41.